CW00696952

We Never Let Go

Tracy Peppiatt

London | New York

Published by Clink Street Publishing 2015

First edition.

ISBN: 978-1-909477-77-3
Ebook: 978-1-909477-78-0

Acknowledgements

A daughter's true story of the pain, loss and heartache her mothered suffered and would never let go of, eventually as time went on and we all grew of age she began to smile.

The identities in this book have been changed to protect the grandchildren of those described, in addition the names of local areas have also been changed for the purposes of confidentiality.

Sally Smith grew up in North-East of England. Sally was born in 1930 to parents John and Dora; they had another daughter Betty who was five years younger. Sally's upbringing was full of happiness and love, however she could never have known what the future would hold.

William Baxter grew up in the North–East of England. Born in 1924 to parents James and Clara they had two other Daughters, Joan and Rita. As a child, suffocated by possession and control, Baxter turned to violence and gambling.

Chapter 1

William Baxter was born on the 19th September 1924. His parents Clara and James had two other children called Joan and Rita. William was born into a working class family living off the good old Hessle Road; his parents were loving, and he was the apple of Clara eye.

Hessle Road was very much a working class area with a lot of men working on the docks as bobbers. If you were lucky enough you would become a trawler man and go out to sea. The women would stay at home and look after the household along with the children.

Each morning Clara would physically pick William up in her arms and carry him to school and seat him at his desk. She would never let his little feet touch the ground. He really was a Mummy's boy until he went into the Navy.

Sally Smith was born on the 15th March 1930. Her parents Dora and John had another daughter, Betty. Sally was born into a middle class family, her father John was a carpenter and they lived in a little two-bedroom house with a front and back garden, which her father kept tidy with borders of flowers. They also had a greenhouse and grew their own tomatoes and vegetables. During the war Sally was evacuated to Dewsbury and her father became a home guard.

Chapter 2
The Beginning

The Beginning

April 10th 1948, Sally Emily shouted 'It's nearly 1 o'clock, he will be here soon! That handsome man of yours… I wonder if he will propose to you today? After all you've been dating for nearly a year.'

'Give over Emily,' Sally replied. 'I don't think he likes me enough to propose.'

'Hello my darling,' a male voice echoed through the store.

'Hello William, were your ears burning? Sally was wondering where you had got to…'

'Oh you fibber,' Sally replied.

'Now girls, please do not fight over me,' William laughed.

'Are you ready Sally?' William winked.

'Yes,' Sally replied, showing her beautiful white teeth.

'I'll just go and fetch my coat,' William continued. 'I have something I want to ask you.'

What could it be? Sally wondered, maybe Emily's right, perhaps William might ask me to marry him?

As they were walking out of the very busy Woolworth store Emily shouted 'Have fun and please don't forget Sally! I want to be your maid of honour!' William turned and looked at Sally's gleaming face.

'What is she talking about? Ignore her Sally replied. 'It was just something she mentioned to me earlier.

'Where would you like lunch today Sally?' William politely asked.

'I don't know, you decide,' sally replied. 'You must be fed up going to Skelton's every day.'

'Ok what about a stroll along the pier? And as it's a nice day maybe we can sit outside if there's a free table?

That would be lovely,' Sally said, putting her arm into William's, he then put both hands in his pockets, walking tall and proud.

'Here we go William,' Sally said, 'a free table at last. Gosh it must be popular, I mean especially with the weather being so nice.'

'Now then love,' a deep voice spoke. 'What I can get you two young lovebirds?

'Leave it out pal,' William replied.

'Oh sorry, the man replied. It's just that I've never seen a couple who look so suited as you two.'

'Maybe so William replied. 'Now please take our order.'

Sally looked up, 'William the man is only being friendly,' she said.

'Well he can go be friendly somewhere else,' came the swift answer.

'Right, now he's cleared off…' William turned to look at Sally, 'I have something I want to ask you.'

'Oh I hope its good!' Sally replied.

'Oh Sally,' came the reply, 'you know how much I love you, ever since the day I walked into Woolworth's, there you were serving a customer with a smile so bright it would light up any grey sky.'

'Sally,' William asked, 'will you marry me? I want to spend the rest of my life with you.

'Oh yes,' Sally replied, 'I love you too.'

'That's settled then,' William beamed. 'Saturday I'll pick you up and take you to meet my parents and two sisters, Joan and Rita before we go to the cinema.'

Sally could not wait for her lunch break to be over, she wanted to hurry back and give Emily her news.

Saturday morning came, Sally was feeling nervous, even though William had already been introduced to her parents. As they drove down Hessle road she gazed at the shops so close together, but also was very aware of the strong smell of fish coming from the docks which made her pull a face.

'Hey Sally don't tell me the snobbery is coming out,' William laughed. 'It's not that bad once you get used to it.'

As they pulled up Sally was aware of the neighbours stood on their doorsteps chatting to one another, the terrace dwellings were very close to each other. 'Mam, Dad!' William shouted as they walk through the door. 'I would like you to meet Sally Smith.'

'Hello Sally,' Clara spoke first, 'pleased to meet you.'

'Sit down love,' James added. 'Joan,' he shouted a little later, 'put the kettle on and make us all a cup of tea will you love? We have a guest, and tell our Rita to come in, it looks like it's going to rain.'

"There you are Rita,' Clara said. 'Come and say hello to Sally.'

'Hello,' Rita replied sheepishly, wondering whom the beautiful long dark-haired lady was standing in her front room. 'Hello Rita,' Sally replied, 'I have heard so much about you and your sister Joan, it's nice to meet you.'

At last William stood up taking Sally's hand. 'Mam, Dad, we have something to tell you, we are engaged to be married.'

'Can Rita and I be bridesmaids?' Joan asked, carrying the tea in from the kitchen.

'Congratulations son!' James shook his hand, and to you too Sally, we welcome you to the family.' Clara however did not look too pleased.

Friday, November 5th 1949: the day had finally arrived. Sally waited anxiously in the room of the registry office with her parents and Betty. Seated on the opposite side of the room were Clara, James, Joan and Rita, William was nowhere to be seen.

'I knew it,' Clara began to moan, 'I told you to go and make sure he had not stopped off at Rayners before we left. You know what he's like - one drink will turn to two, and two to three…' But before Clara could speak, the door opened and William walked in a little worse for wear. He glanced over at his parents with a slight grin on his face, but it was clear his mother was not amused. Despite the early morning hiccup the day went along quite pleasantly. It was now time for Sally and William to leave to start their life together.

Westbourne Terrace

'Well here we are Mrs Baxter, home sweet home. Two rooms in Westbourne Terrace, I know it's not much, but I promise one day we will have our very own Baxter's home… Now then, it's traditional to carry the bride over the threshold.'

With a stagger here and a sway there William picked Sally up.

'Put me down you silly beggar,' Sally laughed, 'you'll crease my dress.'

One fine Saturday morning with William at work on the docks unloading the barrels of fish from trawlers catch the night before, Sally decided to go shopping down Hessle Road. Watching the West Hull people go about their business she stopped at top of Scarborough Street and pondered whether to call in on her in-laws. Before she knew it she was knocking on the door (she could have walked in but people from North Hull would never dream of such thing without waiting to be called in first).

'Good morning mother in law!' Sally smiled.

'I suppose you better come in,' Clare replied.

'It's nice to see you,' Sally smiled.

'Come through to the kitchen,' Clara said, 'there's something I want to discuss with you whilst I make the tea.' Sally started to tremble, she could not understand why her mother in law had taken a dislike to her; all she wanted was to make William her son happy.

Clara reached up to the shelf where a tea caddy was displayed. She took hold of it, then placed it on the table. Sally's shocked impression must have said it all. Clara pulled out a handful of money. Normally you store tea in a caddy, Sally thought. Clara placed the money in Sally's hand and said 'There is, two hundred pounds. I want you take it and leave my son, he will be no good for you.' Sally was so upset, she could not believe it; she loved William with all her heart

'How can you say such a thing?' Sally replied, looking up at her mother in law. 'I came here today to tell you that you and James are going to be grandparents,' Sally spoke with a tear in her eye as she reached for the door.

'You mark my words Sally Baxter you will suffer nothing but heartache,' Clara continued.

August 28th 1952, William was born such a happy baby, with beautiful blonde curly hair. Joan and Rita used to wait at the top of Scarborough Street for Sally, pushing the silver cross pram. Both girls fought hard to be the first to push the pram, and once again the little boy became the apple of his grandparents' eyes.

December 16th 1954: Mary was born, and how different she looked from William; such dark curly hair and dark skin, her tiny body full of hair. When she was first born,

Sally said jokingly 'she looks like a monkey.'

December 27th 1956, James was born, what a content baby - always sucking his thumb and giggling. January 1957, William and Sally were at home. William junior was playing in the yard, Mary meanwhile, quite content sat with her little doll, whilst James was tucked up in his cot asleep. Sally sat in front of the blazing fire, William looked up, 'Hey love, this is interesting… Hull City Council have made an announcement in the paper look…' he said as he walked towards her. 'Sally there is to be a new housing development close to the boarders of Hessle.'

'William shall I pop to the rental office on Monday? Sally smiled, 'and put our name down? You never know, we may be lucky, after all we are overcrowded here.'

'Ok love,' William replied, it's worth a go and you're right, with the old dwellings starting to be pulled down we just might get lucky.'

In March 1957, Sally asked Joan if she would go and view the house as William was working. Dora and John would look after the children, much to their delight (they did not get to see much of their grandchildren as they lived so far away). Sally started to get all excited as she walked up the pathway, 'look how beautiful it is,' she thought to herself, 'I cannot wait to look inside.' As they opened the front door they entered decent sized hallway with a door, which led through to a twenty-foot lounge.

'Oh Joan,' Sally smiled with joy, 'look how spacious it is, we have a bathroom and separate toilet, what a luxury! At Westbourne Terrace the only toilet was outside in the yard.' The bedrooms are spacious Sally,' Joan shouted down from top of the stairs. Sally was so overwhelmed; she could not believe she would soon be in possession of keys and a rent book.

In June 1957, the removal men pulled up, and behind

them in a viva van, were William and Sally.

'I told you one day we would have our own Baxter home love, and here we are,' William smiled.

'I hope the children are not too much for your Mam and Dad,' Sally replied, looking up at the house, 'They will be fine,' she said, 'and you know what our Joan and Rita are like, they have most probably taken over.'

It was six o'clock when the removal men carried in the last piece of furniture. William and Sally started unpacking boxes when a loud knock was heard at the door. 'Who could that be? Sally said.

'I haven't given our address to anyone,' William smiled, walking to answer it.

'Sally,' he shouted. 'It's your Betty.

'Hello love,' Sally smiled. 'Have you come to help us?'

'Yes,' Betty nodded. 'I thought you could do with an extra pair of hands.'

'Ah, thank you Betty, William was just about to find the kettle. Weren't you love?'

'Oh you conned me into that one,' William laughed.

'Sally have you managed to buy any curtains? Betty asked.

'Only for the bedrooms,' Sally replied.

'Well don't worry, I'll make two pairs for the front room and drop them off at the weekend. It won't hurt having newspaper up until then. Thank you Betty you are a good sis,' Sally kissed her on the cheek.

Sally seemed to be happier, especially in the summer. With a large garden Mary and William would play outside and James, still only a baby would be quite content in his pram. Sally was always in the kitchen washing or cooking, so she kept her close eye on the children, in fact the high gate was padlocked, so there was no fear of any harm coming to the children. There was also a brick shed constructed in the garden were toys were stored.

Chapter Three

The Family

September 4th 1959, another baby boy was born – Edward, a very quiet baby who never seemed to cry and was just quiet, happy being fed, changed and placed back in is cot. Mam explain to me when I got older that Edward was a sickly child, now grown up strong.

Oh William, let's hope this is the last of the children, or we'll soon outgrow this property and with you out all the time I find it hard to cope.'

'Stop moaning Sally.'

'Well you never seemed to be at home, you're always out with your friends, coming in at all hours, and I worry you may have had an accident or even worse,' Sally replied.

Two years had gone by and William would continue going to the pub straight from work. Then he started to show signs of resentment, saying things like, 'I wish I had never had met you… And if I had my time over again I would not have had any kids. At one time they both argued so much that Sally took the children back to her parents', and stayed for a few days giving William time to cool off. Then in 1962 something changed…

April 10th 1962, baby Hannah was born, and instantly William took her in his arms and sang 'Because God made thee mine.' The bond between them was very strong. Even her brother William would pay her a lot of attention; they would sit on the sofa and cuddle. One day when Hannah was about four years old, and playing quite happily in the front garden, William could see her clearly as he sat watching television and drinking tea. Cup empty and just about to go into the kitchen he glanced out of the window, but to his horror Hannah was nowhere to be seen.

Frantically he ran to the front door, and there she was, pedalling up the street, 'Hannah,' he shouted as he ran towards her, throwing his arms out. Then he picked her up, 'Oh Hannah,' he cried, 'I thought I had lost you. Hannah kept mumbling 'William/School/William/School.' When Sally returned from Fletchers (she was working there from ten till two after taking Edward and James to school). William, now fourteen and Mary twelve were ok to go alone; their school was but a stone's throw away. Sally was mortified to hear what had happened.

'How could you William?' Sally screamed.

'How could I what?' William replied.

'Take your eyes off her,' Sally sat crying and cuddling Hannah.

'I never,' William replied. 'I went to take my cup to the kitchen and when I looked out she was not there. Do you honestly think I would let anyone or anything hurt my Bain nor any of my kids?'

'Our kids,' Sally mumbled under her breath.

A couple of years had passed and William junior was turning sixteen, he had such a passion for motorbikes and wanted to become a mechanic, which he successfully became. William also had a love for Pigeons and dreamt one day of having his own loft, and maybe racing them but William would not have any of it, always saying birds are bad luck.

Chapter Four

Through Hannah's Eyes

Nana Clara was a proper Hessle Roader; a large lady, always wearing a pinny over her dress. Granddad James on the other hand was a small man but with a broad chest and shoulders. I used to love going to see them because I used to get spoilt. I remember one Saturday morning Mam got me dressed and put me in a brown coat. I used to have to wear a hat, which made my forehead itch. I loved being there with Mam, looking in all the shops, my favourite would have had to have been Woolworths. There used to be a cake counter, you could purchase a slab of cake any size, mam always bought angel cake. We would then pop along to Fletchers, where Mam would buy bacon, sausage, meat pastries. I remember how she would buy duck and make duck ash, it tasted delicious, we would eat it with mash potatoes.

One day Mam and I were in the queue at Fletchers, when all of a sudden the door opened and in walked Nana Clara. I was so happy to see her that I shouted 'Hello Shitty Arse!' Well my Mam went bright red, but all the ladies in the queue started laughing. I was to learn years later that Nana used to call me 'Chitty Bum.'

I remember one of my visits to see Nana and Granddad. Aunt Rita used to live next door, so I would get a chance to see her as well, which was nice. Nana's step was always so clean where she had spent days on her knees scrubbing. There was one door in the front and one leading from the back into the yard. Across the door and what seemed an extremely large keyhole, a very heavy curtain was hung there to try and keep out the draft. Through the next door there was an open fire, a double bed, a small table up against the wall, and laid on top of it was a box of tissues.

The next room was the kitchen/scullery, and then the back door which led to a small yard with an outside toilet. The row of terraced houses was soon to be demolished and my Nana and Grandad were to move into a bungalow within walking distance from where we lived.

One particular day Mam and Nana sat having a good old chat with a cup of tea when I gave out a little cry. I was stood in front of the door talking to the huge key that was in the lock. I was waving my hands about and chatting away when suddenly I fell forwards and bumped my head. Oh, my Nana was cross, she took hold of the key then threw it across the room. I was a right little chatterbox as a child.

When Dad came with us, he would take me to the top of the terrace turn right cross over the road to some loading bays and I would stand watching Granddad haul barrels of fish around. The smell was nasty, but I liked to see Grand-dad at work; he worked so hard.

Aunt Rita lived a couple of doors away, which was nice for Nana and Granddad, she was married with one son called Chris, I remember he used to get very jealous if any of us visited. I suppose he thought he was the only grandchild, I suppose living so close he thought he was, however he was soon going to live a couple of streets away from us. Aunt Joan however lived down Rosemond Street, just off Hessle Road. She owned her home and lived there with her daughter and son and husband Bob. I loved visiting Aunt Joan, because her daughter's bedroom was in the attic and I go up there and explore (I thought they were very posh).

On one of my visits to see Nana Clara, we would find her lying in bed not well at all; she didn't seem to want to talk to anyone. The fire was burning, so the room was quite warm; father told me to go and sit in the other room, which was full of tea, chest ready to take to their new bungalow.

Aunt Rita and Aunt Joan had been called for, I could hear voices, someone had mentioned to fetch the doctor, with that I ran into the room and watched Nana take some tissue out of a box, spit then throw it into the fire. The doctor came and Nana was admitted to hospital. Back home Mam kept busy: washing, ironing, cooking, cleaning, and believe me it was a lot - especially for seven people. Dad kept busy helping granddad get ready for the move, until one day I was sat on the sofa watching the television, Dad stood in front of the window all suited and combing his hair. 'Sally,' he said, 'can you pop to the neighbours?' (We did not have a house phone) 'and call the hospital let the nurses know I will be visiting Mam today.' Within ten minutes Mam came walking back through the door crying.

'What's up Sally?' Dad asked.

Mam replied, 'she's gone William.'

'Whose gone?' Father replied.

'Your Mam.'

'No Dad shouted. 'She can't have, I was just going to see her.'

Mam collapsed to the floor, clinging to Dad's legs. He went crazy, smashing both hands down on the windowpane.

I don't remember the funeral, but ten days later Dad and Aunt Joan went to Granddad's. He was sat in the front room, in a rocking chair, eyes closed with a newspaper laid on his chest. Aunt Joan said to Dad, 'Do not wake him up; let's finish the last box of packing. then wake him.'

'Pop.' Aunt Joan called softly and touched his arm, but he would not wake.

'William,' Aunt Joan shouted, 'quick, come here it's Pop, I cannot wake him.'

Dad walked in from the kitchen. 'He won't wake up.'

Aunt Joan said he had passed away. My Dad was heartbroken, losing them both within ten days of each other. The doctor put his passing down to a broken heart over losing Nana. None of the grandchildren were allowed to go to the funeral, but I do recall the hurt father had inside him; he adored his mother and father.

Chapter Five

Father was never at home, he was always either at work or out drinking and gambling. William Junior's love for pigeons continued and eventually dad gave in and said he could have his very own pigeon loft. He would be in the garden for hours looking after them.

William and Mary were now working, Edward and James were doing what boys do best, it was just me a little girl of eight years old. I loved my younger days at school, I remember one day at primary school the RSPCA brought in a little fox cub and each child in the class was allowed to hold it and had a photograph taken. There I was with my bright blonde hair, squinting at the camera. I also remember that if I brought home a storybook or any paperwork with my name spelt incorrectly dad would complain. It was always Mam that took me to school, never Dad. Remembering when I was at my junior school, Edward and I had a chance to go on a day trip to London. Mam said we could go, and we were both excited but right up to the last minute the trip was not paid for, William stepped in however and paid for us both; there was nothing he would not do for his younger brother and sister.

Mam would often take me to visit Aunty Betty (she stopped coming to our house because of Dad); she used to own a cycle business in the East part of Hull and lived with her husband and two sons, we would get off the bus stop just past the church the shop was situated within a small parade of shops. Once inside you had to climb a flight of stairs to the living quarters, but I liked to stay downstairs where her husband would be repairing bicycles; for some reason I liked the smell of rubber and glue. I used to stand and watch him for a while, I could admire them all... I never had a bike and often wondered why my Aunty would not give me one, but I suppose it was because of money, and unfortunately that's the one thing my mother was short of. She also had a caravan in Bridlington near the east coast where Mam would take Edward, James and I for a day, nothing longer.

On one of my visits Aunty was making a pot of tea, and suddenly realised she had run out of sugar. With no one to fetch any from the shop I had my tea without... I was thirteen years old and to this day I do not take sugar.

We would visit Nana Dora and Granddad John who were very well spoken, they lived in such a beautiful house: two bedrooms, a front room and bathroom, a kitchen with an outer building attached to it and inside a toilet and another bathroom; how different from the terraced houses down Hessle Road. The gardens, how beautiful they looked, with their nicely kept lawns and borders of sweet smelling flowers. A coalbunker was erected in the garden and behind a greenhouse Granddad grew tomatoes.

Every Christmas day Aunty Betty and her two boys would spend their day at Nana Dora's, on Boxing Day Mam, Mary, the boys and I would spend the day together. William always used to say 'No one can make Yorkshire puddings like Nana Dora'. We used to have a lovely day and were always given nice presents by Aunt Betty. Around seven pm William would go and join his friends, as he was old enough then; as the years passed Mary and then James followed. Just before father came to collect us Granddad John would have a shave and get ready for last orders at the Lord Nelson Public House. He would give me a big kiss and rub his stubbly chin against my face, I would laugh. Father used to arrive at ten-thirty, he would beep his horn, but never entered the home. Then we would say good bye to Nana Dora, Edward and I swiftly climbing into the back of the van.

As I sit here writing, Christmas 2013, is approaching and I think back to the Christmases growing up; one in particular that will stay with me forever. It was Boxing Day and Dad collected us as normal, it had been snowing, the sky was so bright, yet it was 11pm when we arrived home and very cold outside; the close where we lived looked liked a skating ring. Other children were already outside, skating up and down. Edward and I joined in the fun, Mam came out about three times and asked us both to come into the house. 'Yes in a minute, we would happily reply.' All of a sudden the window opened and Dad shouted 'In now!' (We soon stopped skating); that was one happy Christmas - I can't believe how the years have passed.

Chapter Six

Growing up Dad worked as a trawler man which meant he was away at sea a lot but being a trawler man's wife meant you had a bit of money. When he was due home Edward and I would wait patiently for the door to open, and for him to walk in. Dad would appear in his white and grey fisherman's jumper, he would always give us both a big silver half crown. All that was soon to change due to the Icelandic war between fishermen; with no more trawlers leaving from Hull a lot of families suffered and a lot of men lost their jobs.

We were ok for a while, Dad got a job as a bobber on the docks and every week Mam and I would go and collect his wages. I hated going because we had to walk under a very low bridge and being near the docks it stank terribly of fish. Once I was out the other side it didn't matter because I could see all the ships, which fascinated me. Mam would keep a tight hold on my hand so nothing happened to me.

Eventually Dad lost his job, due to fighting. It did not take long; things got really bad, especially with no money coming in. Mam had to depend on social security, which must have been so embarrassing for her. There would be times when either Edward or I would need something; on one occasion I had a hole in the sole of my shoe (Dad put cardboard inside). I went to school hoping it wouldn't rain, because not only would my feet get wet my socks would be ruined too.

Dad started to breed Labradors. One dog in particular I remember was called Gunda, she had her own kennel, she was a trained security dog. At the bottom of the garden stood an old workman's hut which was converted into three kennels (then the good old labour ward). the constructed brick shed inside it had a heated lamp… Mam would stay up all night if she had to, just in case the bitch got into difficulty with the puppies. Wonderful Mam was always on hand, bless her. The puppies were so cute, you could never get attached to them, except one day Dad said 'Hannah, I want you to have the pick of the litter and we will keep it'. So I chose a bitch and called her Sherry… At least breeding the Labradors brought in some money.

Whenever I went out with Dad I would fetch Sherry. As soon as I opened the kennel door she would jump up with excitement at the thought of going out. With Sherry in the back of the van we would set out on our travels, often visiting a place called Paull near Hedon, which was the East part of Hull. It was a quaint little village as I recall, with only a few shops, the one I remember the most was the chip shop. Dad would buy fish and chips and we would drive up to what was a small pier just off Main Street and watch the ships going in and out of Hull. I always felt safe with Dad, always protected; when I used to wake up in the morning I would look out of the window, if Dad's van wasn't there I would panic. I wanted to go everywhere with him.

William was working as a mechanic, and James was working for a company called Carmichael's. It was either before or after he started working there that he enlisted in the Navy. I must have only been around thirteen, I can always remember after his home leave I would go with Dad to the station and see him off. I would always cry, mind you that phase didn't last long because he was soon to join the Army and was based in Rippon, North Yorkshire. One night a neighbour knocked on the door, I knew her because sometimes I would play with her children.

'Hello Hannah, is your dad there?' she said.

'Yes, wait I'll go and fetch him.'

'William can you come quick?' the neighbour said. 'James is on the phone and he sounds really upset.'

Dad just ran out of the house, he didn't even stop to put his shoes on.

'Dad,' James cried, 'get me out.'

'What's up son?' Dad replied.

'I want to come home,' James said.

The next day Dad travelled to the Army base and it was said later he was refused entry but Dad being Dad (with his 'I do not give a fuck' attitude) was soon standing in front of the officer in charge laying down his rules. (I was in the army, so I know what it was like; 'if any of you have hurt or bullied my son I will kill you. Now he's coming home with me' that kind of thing). Upon his return, James was very quiet in himself, if anyone asked him what had happened in the Army he would just clam up, he would not even look at his release papers. Years later a couple of the family members wondered if he has been sexually abused.

I went to school with a girl; we were only thirteen and one day, walking home she told me her brother had sexually assaulted her. She did not have anyone to talk to, she was so afraid to tell her father or mother because she feared the outcome. She told me he would call her upstairs into the bedroom, lay on top of her and place his penis between her legs. He never actually inserted himself but he released liquid. I was quite confused at what she was telling me and did not really understand, but now grown up I understand it was bodily fluid. I often wonder what effect it must have had on her growing up. I believe she never had children of her own and could only imagine the impact it made on her life. I know for years I have wondered how she was.

Mary had followed in Mam's footsteps and got a job at Woolworths. One year on my birthday Mam took me into town and we popped into see Mary, she had bought me a pair of pink hot pants with a bib, I must have been only eight years old. I thought they were beautiful.

Mary was a pretty girl with long dark wavy hair and olive skin. I was the blonde child but always wanted to be dark and Mary the opposite, I was told in later years that Mary was so jealous of my hair that she put a basin over my head and cut my hair off. Apparently Mam and Dad were fuming. One day she was at school and a boy in her class was teasing her saying Dad was in prison. His father told him 'no he's not.' Mary replied 'he's at sea'. The boy was right, she went home crying and Dad was in prison, that must have been the time when he came home and I witnessed him burning the furniture. He told Mam it was not his raging bonfire in the garden. He replied 'Hey like Dad's said it's my kennel' (house) 'and I will do what I want.'

Sometimes, if we had enough money Mam and I would go to the Saturday market down Whitefriargate. Even though I liked going out with Mam I didn't like the smell of the rotting vegetables that lay on the floor, especially the cabbage. We would stand with a crowd of people waiting for the butcher to carve a piece of meat, hold it up and say who will give me £1.00? I really felt for Mam.

In the year 1970, Mam never seemed to smile, in fact looking back she became very withdrawn and the doctor would frequent our home a lot. Dad would continue to be Dad but he was always shouting at Mam, sometimes the verbal abuse was horrific and Mam was a nervous wreck around him. Aunty Rita lived a couple of streets away, and for what

I can recall we used to see a lot of her. One day in particular will stay in my memory forever. I was in the front room with Mary, Dad, and Aunt Rita. Mam was seated on the sofa, she just kept rocking and mumbling something when there was a knock on the door and the doctor entered the room, not shortly after him a man in a white coat, they had come to take Mam away, but where to I didn't know. I ran behind the television, which stood, on four legs and started to cry, Aunt Rita would later pick me up and try and comfort me. There seemed to be lots of people talking at the same time, and the doctor saying to Dad 'It will be for the best William, she will get proper help and be taken care of.'

Eventually Mam walked out of the door without saying goodbye, and Dad was left angry. Later that evening Mary washed me and got me ready for bed. The atmosphere was really horrible and all I wanted was my Mam, I suppose I cried myself to sleep.

The next day I do not think Edward or I went to school, but I remember a couple of days later we were at home, there was a knock at the front door, Dad went out the back and walked round to the side of the house to see who it was. I heard loud voices and Dad shouted 'Fuck off; no one is taking my kids nowhere. They are staying with me… I have an older daughter and son who will help me look after them.'

Weeks passed but if felt like months and one morning Mary got me ready and said 'I am taking you out today.' I didn't know where until we arrived. We got on a red bus and seemed to be travelling for about an hour through the countryside, finally it was our stop, we embarked from the bus and approached a long driveway. As we walked down Mary grasped my hand. I watched men and women in white coats coming out of buildings which lined both sides of the driveway. After walking for what seemed a lifetime we finally came to a building that looked like a cricket pavilion. As we entered a nurse approached Mary and asked how could she be of help. I heard Mary say 'We have come to see Sally Baxter, we are her daughters.' The nurse pointed us towards two French doors which led to the outside.

We walked through the doors, Mary still grasping my hand. When we turned left there was a lady sat on a rocking chair; she was most probably harmless, but to me she looked scary. Mam was sat alone, as we approached her she did not seem to recognise us. Mary did her best to talk to Mam and we had a cup of tea. It was quite a warm day, that I remember, there were fields where Mary took me to play, but still with Mam in sight. All of a sudden Mary shouted, 'Look Hannah there's a moo, moo - cow, run!' I did, towards Mam and I saw what I had not seen for a long time, my Mam smile and give a little laugh.

Dad would try his best to look after us, and Mary would continue to help out, but it really was very difficult and I cannot remember him being in the house much, all I could remember was Mary washing me and putting me to bed, she was quite rough with me, if I used to wriggle she would slap my hand.

The months had passed and Mam was coming home, my mother was so beautiful with her long dark hair, but yet when she returned she looked very thin and gaunt and still did not seem to smile a lot. The house became very quiet and Aunty Rita would pop round to see if she could help out in anyway. Looking back it would not surprise me if she had a quiet word with Dad and told him to not lose his temper in anyway or raise his voice, as Mam was still volatile.

I remembering seeing Mam take tablets, she never meant for me to see, I just did. I also remember the day Mam came back from the dentist, she went straight up stairs and locked herself in the bedroom. Dad heated up soup and asked me to take it up to her but she would not open the door, she was crying and telling me to go away. 'What have I done?' I asked. 'Nothing,' Mam said, 'go away.' Later that evening she came downstairs and Dad said 'Are you alright love?' The dentist had pulled out every one of Mam's teeth... She was absolutely devastated her smile had gone.

Slowly Mam was getting better. One day we took a walk to the local shops, it felt really good to have her back, we would have normally gone down Hessle road, but it was one step at a time... As we were walking back through the estate, enjoying a nice pleasant warm day we saw a neighbour Mrs Dixon cutting her grass, she looked up, 'Sally she waved how are you?'

I could tell by Mam's face, she really did not want to stop for a natter.

'I'm fine,' Mam replied.

'I have not seen you lately,' Mrs Dixon said.

'No,' Mam replied. 'I have been a bit under the weather with this flu that has been going around, our Mary has been doing all my shopping.'

Mrs Dixon was a nosey person and could not wait to ask Mam, 'Had she read today's Hull Daily Mail?'

'No,' Mam replied.

'Why,' Mrs Dixon replied, 'there's a man seeking a lady called Sally Baxter, who fits your description. He states they met in Delapole Hospital, but then I thought it couldn't possibly be you... What would you be doing in a mental hospital?'

With that Mam grabbed my hand, quite firmly and said 'Come on Hannah, let's go home.'

As we approached the house you could see Dad sat under the window in front of the television, we walked around to the back door, as we entered through the kitchen I said 'Hello Dad,' but he just stood up and threw the paper at Mam.

'Who the fuck is he?'

'Who's what?' Mam replied.

'There's a bloke in the paper asking the whereabouts of Sally Baxter. Apparently you were in Delapole together. I knew it,' Dad shouted at the top of his voice. 'Electric treatment they gave you. I bet you were having it off with your fancy man.'

'I was not Mam cried, and I do not know who he is.'

'Well he knows you,' Dad said.

Mam started to shake, it was awful to see. She tried to explain, but he would not listen, eventually things calmed down, but I really felt sorry for Mam.

Chapter Seven

Nana Clara was one of eight, all girls. Her sister Ethel was soon to move from her dwelling down Hessle Road; she was to move into a brand new bungalow two streets away from our family home. In a way it was quite nice, because after losing Dad's parents within ten days of each other, I sort of looked upon her as another Nana. I vaguely remember her husband, Great Uncle Jimmy; he used to be a trawler man… He had a couple of fingers missing; apparently he lost them to frost bite and sadly died.

She was a very tall broad lady who constantly took snuff, her handkerchiefs always looked brown (they would if you used as much snuff as she did), her one bedroom bungalow seemed very cosy, with an open fire - the coal used to be stored in a cupboard just before her back door, which led to a communal garden… The front living room was small with just a two-seated sofa, two chairs and a dresser. On top of the dresser stood a glass frame, inside was a photograph of a little girl age about two, she never spoke of her, so I never asked any questions for fear of learning something very sad. Aunt Ethel never left her bungalow, except on a Friday night a black taxi would pull up and take her to a social club down Hessle road where she would enjoy a couple of hours drinking in the company of the old friends she had left behind.

I usually visited her on a Saturday, because that was Dad's gambling day; at exactly twelve noon the television came on, Grandstand (oh I hated that programme). She would say 'Hannah come and sit near the fire, but not too close as you will get corn beef legs.' Basically she meant red marks from the heat. She would often say that I had fine legs; lots of our conversations would be about the good old days and Nana Clara. She would go on, and say Nana Clara would have been proud of me. She told me that my Dad respected his Mam so much, that she was the only one who could tell him off, and that he would do exactly as she said.

Dad would say, 'If Aunty offers you anything to eat, take it, but say you will have it later…' Once I returned home I was instructed to throw it in the dustbin. He had such funny ways, he would not eat or drink anything unless Mam made it, and back in those days' people who took snuff found it a substitute for tobacco, and Dad hated anything to do with smoking.

Things were still very tough, and with money short, especially for Mam she would take the only suit dad had and pawn it; how embarrassing, especially coming from a middle class family, but then again, I don't suppose she would have told her parents. On many occasions Mam would go and ask Aunt Ethel to lend her a few pounds and promise to pay her back when she received her money from social services. Aunt Ethel made you wait a long time for an answer, I think she like to see you beg. Dad was her nephew but she knew no matter what he had in his pocket, he would either keep it for himself or gamble it away (looking back I know why Aunt Ethel was glued to the chair), she used to sit on her purse, which was full of green pound notes - that was a lot of money back then.

Chapter Eight

One day Mam and I returned from shopping only to see William Junior crying, and Dad in a foul mood.

'What is wrong Mam?' Asked William.

'They're all dead,' William howled.

'Who's dead?' Mam said.

'My pigeons,' he cried.

'Calm down, William and tell me what's happened.'

'All my pigeons Mam, I went to feed them and their necks had been rung.'

'I done it,' Dad bellowed from his chair. 'They're fucking bad luck, I'll never have any good luck while they're in the garden.'

'You bastard,' Mam said.

I looked up in horror, I had never heard my Mam say 'bloody' never mind a swear word.

'Don't tell me you've been gambling again,' Mam looked at Dad.

'Shut your fucking mouth,' he replied, 'and go with your fancy man.'

'I have got no fancy man,' she replied, and with that Dad stood up and slapped Mam across the face.

He hated anyone talking back at him; he was the boss of

the house and believed we should all do as he says… Eventually things calmed down and Mam started to cook our tea. We never ate together, Dad used to sit at the table in the kitchen, and the rest of us would have it on our laps.

When Mam was in the kitchen cooking none of us were allowed to go in. Dad really had funny ways; he would say to us 'wash your hands' (to this day I wash my hands constantly). We could never touch the newspaper until he had read it first, we were never allowed to sit downstairs in our nightwear, he had his own knife and fork and crockery and no one else was allowed to use any of it.

We couldn't afford family holidays, so Dad would take Mam, Edward and I to Withernsea or Scarborough, drop us off, then say he would collect us later, but he never hung around and later I would find out he had found a bookmakers and gone gambling. You really couldn't tell what mood he would be in until we got back in the van. You knew things were alright when he would say 'Let's get fish and chips to take home for supper.'

Things seemed to be getting back to normal and Dad's love of Labrador breeding continued. Well at least it brought some money in, We always had a meal on the table, we never went to bed hungry, just cold, as we were very short on bedding and used to wrap up in coats to keep warm. Infact the bedroom did not look like one at all, it was just an old bed, no wallpaper, no carpets or wardrobes to hang clothes. Edward and I shared a bed and would fight over the coats, even William slept on an old mattress with one pillow, one blanket and no carpet. He liked his sleep, he was known to go to bed on a Friday night and not get up until Monday morning.

On Saturday mornings I would creep into William's bare room and say 'William please can I have some pocket money?' He would reach into the pocket of his trousers, which lay on the bare floorboards, and give me whatever he had.

Then in 1971 we had a stroke of luck; Dad found a job in security, he would work from 3pm till 12pm; his job was to patrol a council estate in North Hull with a dog. No tenants occupied the properties, they been moved out so the council could refurbish the houses and turn them into suitable living accommodation.

On a cold winter's night Dad was on his rounds patrolling, and he heard a noise coming from behind a storage container. Dad shouted 'Who's there?' But he got no reply. Once again Dad shouted and the noise appeared to come from behind one of the terraced properties. All of a sudden there was the sound of breaking glass. He shouted at the top of his voice, 'I have a dog with me! Come out or I'll send the dog in. You have been warned!'

Still no one appeared, so in went the dog. Gunda locked jaws with the culprit; the screams were terrible as her teeth bit into his groin. Dad shouted 'Leave' and Gunda retreated to his side. The man was badly hurt, Dad called for ambulance and also the police, the man was taken to Hull Royal Infirmary. Before he went into theatre it was said his own mother had said 'It serves you right; you should not have been there in the first place, you were trespassing.' No charges were made towards Dad or the company.

William was happy again after buying new pigeon stock, and with money coming in life seemed normal for awhile. Mary had made a friend call Janet who worked with her, she   lived locally in Gipsyville. She would often go straight to Janet's after work for her tea, with Dad's permission of course. That summer Janet's parents had planned a holiday to the Isle of Man and asked Mary if she would like to go with them. Mary said she would love to but would need to ask Mam and Dad permission. With a lot of persuasion Dad said yes, so off she went for two weeks. I didn't miss her because by the time she came home from work I was already tucked up in bed.

Chapter Nine

Christmas 1971

Edward and I were looking forward to Christmas, which was to be the last happy one for a long time. I can still smell the aroma coming from the kitchen where Mam would spend hours baking mince pies, lemon curds and jam tarts. We never had Christmas cake because no one liked it and I think only Mam liked Christmas pudding. About a week before, Edward and I would help with the decorations, which were paper chains… You had to lick one end, then loop them together. We could never afford the fancy ones, but there were still very nice ones. We used to have a small tree, which stood in the left corner of the front room, no lights though, that was another luxury we could not afford.

We used to rent the television from a company called Telebank. You put fifty pence in the meter and it gave you eight hours of viewing. Every four to six weeks a man would call to empty the box, and if there was money left over Mam could either take it or put it towards items you could purchase from their catalogue. To be honest the majority of the time Mam needed the money. I used to sit for hours looking through the catalogue asking for things.

Christmas Eve came… I believed in Father Christmas but

Edward used to tease me and say he didn't exist. We went to bed early but I opened my eyes to see Mam stumbling around and opening doors. When I woke on Christmas morning I ran down the stairs to find Father Christmas had been and left me my own desk. On top stood a little doll, which I still have thirty-eight years later, in her original blue dress, with no shoes and no pants. I think I must have lost them. I will never throw the doll away; it reminds me of the happy times with Mam.

Edward seemed happy with what he was given, but to be honest I cannot remember, except there were two games, Kaplunk and Mouse Trap, 'To Edward and Hannah - love from William'. We argued so much over Kaplunk because I would take the marbles outside and lose them playing games with my friends.

It's funny really, I could never remember William James or Mary being there on Christmas day just Mam Edward and I. Mam would be in the kitchen slicing the turkey which she had cooked the day before and preparing the vegetables. Dad would just sit in his chair and watch television; it was as though he was letting us have one decent day of the year. On Boxing Day, as normal Dad dropped us off at Nana Dora's.

Once Christmas was over everything went back to normal: Dad was working at his security job, the house hold was plodding along, until one Sunday morning Mary was sat on the sofa watching television, her favourite bottle of lemonade at her side. I was sat on the chair playing with my dolly and Mam was in the kitchen attending to her daily chores. Suddenly the door opened and in walked Dad. Mary looked up, 'Dad?'

'Yes love,' Dad replied. 'I want to go back to the Isle of Man.'

'You can love, for a holiday.'

'No Dad,' Mary replied. 'I want to live there.'

'Over my dead body,' Dad replied. 'You aren't living nowhere, except here.'

Chapter Ten

A Terrible Night

Mary had continued to work at Woolworths, but in her spare time she used to babysit for Mr & Mr Williams who lived two streets away. They had two adopted children, Mandy and Stephen, because they could not have children of their own.

One night in December 1972, with Christmas only seven days away, the front room covered in paper chains and a tree in the corner, as normal I was getting all excited, wondering what Father Christmas would bring me. With Dad at work, all of us (Mam included) safely tucked up in our beds well (at least I thought we were), until we awoke to hear Dad shouting at the top of his voice, 'Get up! Get up all of you! Now!'

Mam was the first to answer. 'What on Earth is it? It's half twelve at night.'

'I don't care what bastard time it is,' Dad shouted, 'get up… I bet you knew she planned this.'

'Who planned what?' Mam replied.

'Mary, she's gone.'

'Where?' Mam asked.

'She fucked off, she left home,' Dad's voice echoed, being young I didn't know what was happening, however I had seen Dad fly off the handle before… I just started to cry.

Dad would return each evening from work, he would go

into the kitchen, make a cup of tea, read the paper, before bedding down on the sofa - he never went to bed. This particular evening he had changed his routine, he walked straight into the hallway, took off his car coat, and there it was, the crispy white envelope laid on the concrete floor (we never had a hallway carpet) it looked as though it was placed there and not put through the letter box.

Dad was crazy with anger, Mam was crying - how could Mary just leave and not say anything? Dad said, 'she must have gone back to the Isle of Man.'

But he kept blaming Mam, goodness knows what the neighbours must have thought of all the noise (to be honest Dad never cared what people thought), the house was his kennel as he used to say.

Daylight came, and Dad went to the police station, he reported Mary missing and told them she was under age, only seventeen years old, forgetting however that only two days earlier she had turned eighteen. Dad explained to the police about the Isle of Man and apparently the next day the police found her, but could not bring her home; she was old enough now to live away. She asked the police not to tell Dad were she was. I do not hate her but shall never forgive her for the next nine years of hell she put us all through, especially Mam.

She planned her escape well; when she had her babysitting duties for the Williams she would take some of her clothes round and store them there, in fairness they should not have encouraged her. She also asked Woolworths to arrange a transfer to the Isle of Man. One big mistake she nearly made (and if she had maybe Mam's life would have been different). On the night she was to leave she crept into the bedroom and said goodbye, but then paused for a moment, thinking she could take James with her. I love all my brothers but Mary seemed to show James more attention, they even went to the same school together - she would be there for him at playtime, dinner time - when she left school and started work James became withdrawn for a long time.

Mary knew this was impossible, because he was two years younger. If the police had caught up with her she would have had to have to come home. She walked out of the room down the stairs, placed the envelope on the floor and walked out.

It was an awful time, Dad would visit the Williams and insist they told him where she was, but of course they denied all knowledge, he also went to the parents' home of her friend Janet to find they had given permission for their daughter to leave.

'Where is she? Where's my daughter?' He banged on the door and shouted through the letter box, 'I swear if you do not tell me, I will petrol bomb your fucking house and blow you all up you bastards.'

He would drive through the streets of Hull at all hours, and take Mam with him, he drove through parks and if he saw anyone seated on a bench he would tell Mam to get out and check to see if it was Mary. The police had said nothing to Dad about her whereabouts, that she was safe in the Isle of Man, so in Dad's eyes she could have been anywhere.

The next day after the dreaded envelope was found, Dad went to work as normal, but what happened next only added more sadness and heartache for Mam to cope with. He was patrolling the rounds as normal, but could not get Mary or the events of the night before out of his head, he decided to call it a night, but it was only nine o'clock, and he did not finish until twelve pm. He put Gunda in the car and made his way home, knowing full well he would soon be going out again with Mam to continue searching for Mary. It was hope-less - she had gone and he would have to try and accept it.

The following day he returned to work to find the area manager waiting for him.

'Where were you last night William?' The manager asked.

'Here,' Dad replied. 'Where do you think I was?'

'Well I called at nine thirty and you were nowhere to be found.'

'I must have been out on my rounds,' Dad said, knowing damn well he had left early. The manager had kept on and on and told Dad he would not get paid for the shift. Dad jumped up in his face and argued with him, the manager was so frightened, he headed for the door Dad grabbed hold of him and pushed him against the wall, but he tried to escape. Dad was too strong and put all his body weight against the door, the manager was trapped behind and could not breathe, finally Dad moved away, but was sacked on the spot.

With only five days to Christmas, Mam had no money, so she went along to social security office to ask for an emergency grant, even though it was Dad's fault they had no money. He would wait in the van; he was too proud a man to beg; however Mam returned crying.

'They will not give us any money, William,' she said. 'I have to go back after Christmas to fill out paperwork.'

Dad started shouting again, 'the fucking bastards,' he said, 'that seemed to be his favourite word.

'What are we going to do? Mam cried, 'I still have food to buy.'

What a hero... William junior, he stepped in, buying meat, fruit, vegetables nuts etc.

Chapter Eleven

January 1972

It was a new year back at school. I hated school, I was told if anyone asked about Mary I was to say she was at work, but of course it was a lie. The whole family was shocked at what she had done, but at the same time we had to carry on. I found a photograph of her when she used to work at Woolworths, and from time to time, without Dad knowing I would get it out and look at it, though we were never allowed to mention her name. A couple of years had passed, and each Christmas when Mam and I were putting up the tree, she would place a small fluffy dog upon it and whisper 'Happy Christmas Mary, whereever you are.' I had to turn away as it broke my heart seeing Mam so upset.

Dad would go out in between Christmas and New Year, and the next day Mrs Smith, one of our neighbours would knock and say 'Sally, William is on the phone.' We never had a phone, we could not afford it. Mam would ask, 'Where are you?' And he would say, 'I am in Motherwell,' which was Scotland. Mam would ask 'When are you coming home? And to be honest, it was never until after the New Year. He would stay drinking with his crooners, that's what friends called each other back then.

He was never at home, always out drinking till all hours.

His temper got more and more aggressive, he was gambling all the time, it seemed the only time he was happy was when he had money in his pocket. Mam was the one that kept the home clean; she was the one that worried about us all. I felt so sorry for her, but I was only a child and could do nothing; we all had to obey what Dad said. We lived in a three-bedroom house, no carpets except one in the front room, a sofa that had holes in the arms, no wallpaper except in the front room... I even remember having to wipe my bottom on newspaper. Sometimes we would have newspaper up at the windows, it was tiring telling people we were decorating. We never used the front door because of the embarrassment; you always came and went from the back door. Still sharing a bed with my brother, and wrapping up in coats, which to me was normal - the kitchen was very bare, just a table, one chair and a cooker, no fridge, we kept what food we had in a pantry, but in the summer it used to be swarming with ants because sugar was kept there.

Mam and Dad never slept together, Dad was always downstairs on the sofa because we had only had one gas fire. In winter, when it was really cold we used to pull the sofa and chairs up to keep us warm. I was loved by both my parents and no matter how bad Dad was, I just thought it was normal. Sometimes Mam would go to bingo down Hessle road and when Dad would go and pick her up I would go with him at half ten; chucking out time. I would get out the van and wait at the bottom of the stairs. I loved it; as soon as Mam saw me she would give me her beautiful smile. As we climbed back in the van Dad would say, 'Have you done any good? And if Mam said no, he would say, 'our luck's in bastard China.'

Saturdays came and Mam would go shopping, then to bingo. I could not go with her, no children were allowed. Sometimes I would go with her and bring back what few groceries she could afford, or I would pop in and see Aunt Joan. She would get the tin down and give me a blue ribbon wafer biscuit. Norman Collier's son had a shop across the road from aunt Joan. Sometimes I would pop in and buy sweets to take back home. Grandstand would come on at twelve noon, the first hour was alright, but as soon as the horse racing started I would go and see Aunt Ethel. Dad would be gambling, and he was a bad loser. If James was in the room he would tell him to go and put a bet on, he was not old enough to enter the bookies, so would wait outside and ask some passing bystander to place it for him; goodness knows what they must have thought if the horse did not win. Dad called him the jinx of the family, even though he tried really hard to please Dad.

One Saturday I made my way to Aunt Ethel's. Not knowing what the day would bring, I tried to stay out as long as I could, but sometimes I would sneak back home go straight upstairs and gaze out of the window, waiting for Mam to appear at the top of the street. As soon as she was in sight I would run to meet her, as I approached, Mam would say, 'Everything ok? I would reply, 'No, it's snowing.' That meant Dad had lost his money. He would take a newspaper and tear it into pieces and throw it all over the house, not only that, he would take a pen and write on the front room wall 'This fucking bastard house, I hate it.'

It was always Mam who had to pick up the pieces and clean the walls not just once but a hundred times; on Saturday evenings after tea Mam would sit down and take out a packet of ten number six cigarettes and light one up. Dad would say, 'You smoking again? It would be Mam's first one of the day. If he could have a go at Mam he would, there was no pleasing him, he would kick off about anything and everything.

Every Saturday night Mam would get out the washing from the machine with a wringer attached to it. Dad would be either laid on the sofa or in front of the fire, the match of the day would be on the television, and he would shout 'You fucking washing again? I can't hear the bastard telly.' It didn't matter that poor Mam stood for hours washing all our clothes. Sometimes I would go into the kitchen and help out, but she worried that I'd get my hands caught in the wringer… getting it dry was a bigger problem too; ok in the summer but terrible in the winter. We had a washing line in the garden but Dad would not let Mam hang out our underwear, because next door lived two boys, and he did not want them seeing what we wore.

Chapter Twelve

Mam went into hospital for a hysterectomy; Edward and I were still attending school, Mary was no longer around. William and James were at work; it was left to Dad to look after us. He would shout to wake us up in the morning and give us a bowl of Scots Oats porridge, it tasted horrible - with a texture as thick as glue because he made it with water instead of milk. We were also given a bottle of Silver Top milk to drink, now known as skimmed milk.

Edward and I were in the kitchen, and the small window was open, he was getting something out of the pantry. Edward, I asked, 'What does spread eagled mean?'

'Who said that?' Edward replied.

'I heard it outside,' I said.

'Do not say that word,' he said. 'It's not nice.'

'What does get fucked mean?' I continued.

'Stop it,' Edward said. 'If Dad hears you he will go mad. With that I turned around and there Dad was resting on the ledge outside, looking through the window which was also open at the top. He shot through the door

'What did you say to your brother?' he shouted at me. He asked me three times before I replied. Edward tried to calm the situation saying I heard it outside. Dad grabbed me and put me over the arm of the sofa, then he slapped my back-side so hard I never said it again.

Mam was home from hospital and needed plenty of rest. For twelve weeks she was not allowed to rush about or lift anything heavy. A round Hoover had been advertised on the television, so Dad said 'I will buy one of them Sally, because it floats and it will be easy for you.'

The nights were drawing in and Dad would be out till all hours sometimes, he would not come home till the next day, but to be honest I think Mam preferred it that way because he could sleep his booze off elsewhere. If he came home the same night with fish and chips you knew he had had a successful day and was in a good mood. On one occasion we were all in bed, at about two o'clock in the morning Mam was awoken by the police knocking on the door, apparently Dad came out of a nightclub, got in his van and forgot to switch on the lights, so they followed him. He wasn't drunk, but when the police stopped him he was very abusive, so they locked him in the cells for the night. He was like a raging bull, the officer informed Mam that she had come to collect Dad's tablets. Mam told the police he wasn't taking any medication. 'He will be having you run around after him,' she said, but the police had to double check, because they did not want to be responsible if anything happened to Dad while he was in their custody.

Mam had gone back into hospital to have her bunions removed, the surgeon decided to operate on both feet. In one way Mam thought it was a good idea, but on the other hand she worried how we would manage. I went with Dad to visit her, and before Mam was discharged she had to practice walking up and down the hospital stairs; this was to ensure Mam could manage to get to the bathroom once home.

One sunny day Dad said, 'I tell you what Sally, Hannah, you and I will go out for the day.' I wanted to take Sherry, we all climbed in the van and set out. Dad drove to a quaint little village called Pocklington just outside Hull, once there, what did he do? Find a bookmakers and stayed in there for about four hours. My poor Mam was on crutches, with both legs in plaster above her knees and me only a young child.

When he finally finished gambling, we all climbed back into the van. Sherry had been on her own all the time. I wanted to asked if we could stop on the way back, so she could have a little run but dared not ask, just in case he had lost all his money. I don't think Mam was too happy either, but kept quiet until eventually Mam said 'I cannot believe you drove us all that way so you could go gambling. All Hannah and I have done is walk round and round and I am very tired and thankful it did not rain.'

Something I Shall Never Forget

Like a man possessed, the door opened and in walked Dad with a face like thunder. Only Mam and Edward were at home. He looked at Mam and started verbally abusing her, he seem to get louder and louder; the things he said still haunt me. He called her a whore and told her to 'Go and get fucked from her fancy man.' He was a raging bull; I have never seen him like it before. Mam shouted back at him to 'shut up and drop dead'. All of a sudden he grabbed her by her hair, I went towards him to tell him to leave Mam alone, but he pushed me and I fell back on the chair and the chair went over. Edward shouted, 'Get off my Mam and sister.'

'Fuck off you're not even mine,' Dad shouted back.

Mam called Dad a bastard, with that he took Mam's head and smashed it against the wall, he kept on smashing and smashing her head, he picked up the Hoover and with such force threw it against the wall where it left a dent. Mam managed to escape from him and took Edward and I to a neighbour, Mrs Jones who said 'If he comes here I will stab him'. Mam kept saying 'I can't stand it no more, I need to get away.'

Mrs Jones called the police, and a man from social services came and collected us but Mam would not get in the car at first, in case Dad was outside. We were then taken to a battered wife's hostel down Beverly Road. There we were greeted by a woman who showed us to a room; it was quite dark, so we just got into bed. The next morning I awoke to see other mothers and their children in the room, which was lined with multiple beds on either side. We were shown into a room where people sat eating breakfast, we too were given some but I could not eat, I just kept crying, 'I want my Dad, I want my Dad,' not looking up at the other people, a man came to see Mam about what had happened the night before, and to sort out some personal belongings but that meant going home to collect them. Mam was afraid he would be there waiting for us, and not knowing what mood he would be in and what he would do we eventually got into the car on our way home to collect some things. As we turned the corner, we saw him stood against the front door. It was obvious he was looking for us and wondering where we had stayed the night before.

'Drive on,' Mam said. 'Please do not stop.'

But I screamed, 'I want my Dad,' as I looked back out the car window he saw me. The man drove round again but this time when we approached the house Mam said, 'Stop,' and got out of the car, but told Edward and I to stay put.

Dad walked towards her, 'Sally,' he said.

'Don't touch me, William, please don't touch me.'

I could see Mam crying and shaking.

'I am sorry, please do not leave me,' he continued.

I watched as they talked for awhile, eventually we got out of the car and all went into the house and the social worker drove away. Mam stood still, not knowing what would happen next. Dad had tears in his eyes.

'I swear I shall never lay a hand on you again,' he said. 'I have just come back from Aunt Ethel's and told her what I'd done and that I was scared that I lost you and the bains.

'If you ever touch me again William I will leave you, and not come back you,' Mam cried. 'You really hurt me, I cannot take it anymore.'

Chapter Thirteen

I loved going with Mam and Dad to visit friends just outside Huddersfield, a little village called Cleckheaton; they had a beautiful home and always gave me a box of chocolate brazil nuts. They owned horses, I had such a passion for horses when I was growing up, so much so that one Friday, Dad said, 'Hannah, I have a surprise for you.' I kept nagging him till eventually he gave in and said, 'I've bought you a pony.' I was so happy, 'Can we go and see it?'

'Yes,' Dad said, 'just let me have my cup of tea.'

Ramona was light chestnut; she was in the stables, at Long Risen which was on the way to Hornsea, a seaside resort. How lovely she looked, and all mine. I couldn't wait to ride her, but Dad had to buy me a riding hat and boots first, but no whip… He thought it was cruel to use one.

One Sunday I was out riding with the other children, when all of a sudden Ramona bucked and threw me off. The horse behind had tugged on her tail. Dad sold her not long after; he said she was too flighty, I was so upset.

Dad kept his promise and never raised his hand to Mam, but he was still gambling and staying out till all hours. Edward started to learn to box, Dad was very proud of him and used to accompany him whenever he could. He took me once to watch him fight in Rotherham, I was proud of my brother, but did not like it if he took a punch from his opponent.

Edward promised Mam that one-day, when he had enough money he would have a stone fireplace built for her and he kept his word. As I was growing up I started to become jealous of Edward, he seemed to be getting all the attention. I remember William once saying to him 'You win this fight and tonight I will buy you a new tracksuit'. Some nights I would wait up for him to see if he had won.

I loved all my brothers but I felt extra close to Edward. I think it was because we were close in age and he always looked out for me, he was never greedy. One night he came home after winning a fight and gave me money. There was also a time when I nagged Mam for a leather coat, but she could not afford it so Edward bought it for me.

Angel of all angels our Mam; she would continue to look after us all, keep the house clean and manage with what money Dad gave her. She would even help aunt Rita, yes Dear Aunt Rita; she became a mother again fifteen years after her first son. Mam was always there to help, remembering the night Aunty came home from the hospital with her baby son Matthew in a carry cot. He had filled his nappy, but it was Mam that changed it, and from that day Mam cared for him, she even took him to his first day at school. Matthew was two years old when Aunty became ill; she sadly passed away when he was eighteen. I have always looked upon Mathew as my baby brother and always will. Mam also cared for Aunt Ethel, Mam never seemed to sit down, but you never heard her complain.

I never went to school much, because I was bullied, the board man used to come round and ask why I was not attending; Dad would simply say 'because I have kept her off'. Mam would get upset, but I hated school and at the back of my mind I worried that one-day I would come home and neither Mam nor Dad would be there.

Waking up one morning I asked Mam, 'Where has Dad gone?'

'There is a letter on the mantle piece for you,' she replied.

Dear Hannah,' it read. 'I have had to go away for a while. Be a good girl and you will get your bike,' (I always wanted a bike), 'love Dad.' He always promised me a bike, but we could not afford it. I cried my eyes out. Mam said he had gone back to sea... I used to sit looking out of the window for hours, waiting for him to turn the corner, the fishing trip did not last long as he was thrown off the ship for fighting.

Dad was always fighting when I was a little girl, he would come home with blood on his knuckles... No one was allowed to ask questions. It was well known that when Edward had a boxing match, Dad would be arguing or fighting with someone in the crowd. I was a bridesmaid once for a friend, at the reception one of the guests told me he had witnessed Dad throwing a snooker ball through a television set, because his horse did not win. It seemed everyone knew of William Baxter's temper. I dare not repeat this to Dad he would have gone looking for him.

I managed to get myself a Saturday job in a shop local to where we lived. It sold just about everything. Shopkeepers Christine and Christopher were very kind to me, and I loved working for them. Mam would frequent the shop a lot at first. I thought it was to see how well I was doing, but then I found out later Mam used to get credit, so each week she would pay her bill, then get more shopping. Eventually I left and worked in the fruit and veg shop across the road. I was always left on my own, Maxine who owned the shop was going through marital problems.

On one occasion Mam came into the shop. My brother James was upstairs with Maxine kissing and cuddling. James was so handsome; all the women fell for him. Mam would give me her order, but I always made sure I gave her extra potatoes or a vegetable, that's how it was - you looked after your own.

I promised Mam that when I got older, I would make sure she had whatever she needed. It was not fair that such a wonderful Mam who gave her love and time to everyone had to go without and suffer. I saved up fifty five pounds once, and bought some cushion flooring for the kitchen, as the floor was still bare concrete. Mam gave me the money back.

Why were we living the way we did? We had nothing but the love of our Mam, Dad loved us, of course he did, but he had a terrible way of showing it. He was too possessive; if I walked down the street and their were workman around, he used to watch, just in case they would say anything, and then he would attack. I remember one day I was talking with a friend on the front, and two boys walked up. One of them called my friend a slag, the next thing I knew Dad was shouting, 'Sally take Hannah to the doctors. I want to make sure she is a virgin.' For goodness sake… I was sixteen.

There was another occasion when a boy knocked on the door and explained that Mr Andrews was on the field and wanted to talk to Dad, straight away Dad put on his shoes and before the poor man could explain, Dad nutted him. The man had brought the two pounds that his son owed our William, he knew of Dad's reputation and clearly did not want any trouble.

Aunt Rita's oldest son was having trouble at school from one of the teachers, and Dad went to sort it out, as his own father could not be bothered. It was said the headmaster had to lock the teacher in a classroom for his own protection.

I would be playing in the close, and then a police car would pull up, and Dad would get out, but the funny thing was he fell off the bus drunk, and the police recognised him and brought him home. I loved my Dad but also feared him. We were coming back from a day out with Sherry in the back of the van, from the north part of Hull, not far from Nana Dora's, when all of a sudden Dad said, 'Listen to me, my brakes have failed. I am going to slow the van down as best I can with the hand brake, fingers crossed we get across this junction. I will get as close to the grass verge and when I say jump, jump onto the grass.'

'No Dad, I will not I am not leaving you,' I replied. I kept my word, and eventually the van stopped.

Another time Dad came home after a day of gambling, he had something to eat, then fell asleep… When he woke he went to fetch Sherry from the back of the van, but she was not there. While he had been in the bookies, he had left the window open a bit, she must have jumped out, it was very unlike her. I was upset she had gone. He had to retrace his steps as he had been in a bookies up North Hull. Dad went to see if he could find her, but it was impossible.

Then one day Nana Dora had told Mam she had been to the shops, and on her walk back she saw a black Labrador that looked well fed, roaming on the playing field, Dad was soon scouring the area, there she was, but not on her own; a rough looking man was with her. 'Excuse me Pal,' Dad said.

'Yeah,' the man replied, 'the dog is mine.'

'I don't think so,' the man replied.

Dad turned and called out, 'Sherry,' and she ran to him, all excited.

I will call the police the man said.

'She is mine, call the fucking police,' Dad said. 'Now fuck off, I am taking the dog.'

I was so pleased to see her, I cuddled her, and she licked my face - the fortunate thing was she had been looked after. Dad reckons she did not jump out of the window, the man must have taken her.

Chapter Fourteen

Mam had a very dear friend, Hilary who lived a few doors away from us, her husband Bill would sometimes help me with my homework. Hilary worked at a local fish factory. When she was on the two to ten shift, she could not sleep, so at about half ten pm, when she came home, Mam and I would go and see her for a few hours. I liked Monday nights, because we used to sit down with a cup of tea and a biscuit and watch Prisoner Cell Block H. Some nights she would bake fresh bread, and used to let me help her ,the only thing I didn't like was all the smoking she did. Well, it was her house, but she never seemed to use an ashtray, always letting the ash fall on the carpet and rubbing it in with her foot.

On a weekend, when it got dark, Dad and I would drive around the country lanes, looking for fields with Hay in them. Dad would park up, and ask me to keep looking out while he would go into the field and help himself to the bundle that was used for the kennels. I suppose back then it was stealing, but to me it was normal way of life, however we were all brought up to keep quiet.

I remember one morning in particular, waking up and there was a terrible smell, at first no one knew where it was coming from, Dad found a newspaper parcel on the hallway floor - it had been posted through the letter box. When Dad opened it, it was full of dog poo... He went ballistic. Apparently there was a women who lived at top of the street, and she had found the poo on her path, she knew Dad bred Labradors, so thought it must have been one of Dad's dogs and decided to give it back. How very wrong she was, Dad took the parcel, knocked on her door and threw the lot over her, luckily the police didn't come because she was at fault.

Our dogs were never out roaming the streets, and if Dad found any dog poo on our path or garden, he would shovel it up and throw it back into the street, Mam used to get annoyed, but Dad would say, 'It's not my fucking shit.' Any rubbish that was on our property that did not belong to us got thrown back.

Dad would drive all over the country attending dog's shows. He had a friend who accompanied him called Sharon, she would walk the dog up and down in front of the judges, over the years he won a lot of rosettes. The only show I attended with him was Hull show, in East Park, but he never entered. That year we had a lovely day, especially watching the horse jumping.

One day the sun was shining and it was very hot, Mam was in the kitchen attending to her daily chores, the dogs would not stop barking. I mean if one barked they all barked, by that time we had five of them.

'William,' Mam said, 'the dogs are barking, can you please tell them to be quiet?'

'Let them bark,' Dad replied.

'Think of the neighbours,' Mam said.

'Fuck the neighbours,' was his reply.

All of a sudden a man shouted, 'Will you keep them dogs quiet?'

Dad jumped up, grabbed a hand shovel from the shed,

went next door and attacked the man who lived there. His wife was screaming, and Dad nearly took his head off.

Another horrific day, he was watching the television as normal and gambling when his horse fell, so with cup in his hand he threw it straight through the front room window, and yet none of us was allowed to say anything. Mam had to call the council the next day and make an excuse as to why it was smashed. He would slam doors so loudly that once he pulled a door off its hinges with one hand. When I started working I bought Mam two nice pine doors with eight small panes of glass, he even smashed two of them.

'Dad,' I would say, 'can we have the house decorated?'

'Nobody is coming in this bastard house,' he would say; the house that he hated.

There was a detached house at the top of our street and one day, as we were driving past Dad told me a story... You see that house Hannah? That should have been mine, well ours; the council promised it to me, I had my name down for it, but the fucking cunts gave it to someone else. It would have been ideal, out of the way, with enough room for my kennels. He would always say to me, 'If I had my way I would have bought a big mansion,' with enough rooms for all his kids and grandchildren to live in, that's how possessive he was.

One Saturday morning I wanted to go on Hessle Road with Mam. I had seen a denim skirt with buttons up the front, all the girls were wearing them. Mam said 'Hannah stop nagging, I have not got any money, please just go to the shop and fetch me two bottles of milk.'

I set off all miserable and in tears. As I crossed the road near the bookmakers (yes the shop I grew to hate so much) I looked down and there was a five pound note. My first thought was yes! I can now buy the skirt, but then I looked round to see if anyone had dropped it, the answer was no, so I bought the milk and ran all the way home.

'Mam, look what I found.'

'Where?' Mam asked.

'Outside the bookies. Can I have my skirt please?'

Mam said, 'it's not yours really.'

'But if there was no one around to claim it…'

'Then yes,' she said. Mam took me to Boyes on Hessle Road and I bought one, four pounds ninety nine and a half it cost. I wore that skirt day and night.

Dad would take the dogs out for a walk early in the morning, and after he would sit on the wall at the top of the street. He sat down as normal. When he spotted a briefcase in the telephone box he opened it, and there must have been two thousand pounds inside, he brought it home and found out it belonged to the local barber. Dad gave it back to him, he called the barber 'all the robbing bastards' under the sun as he got no reward, not even a free haircut.

My Dad, I loved him very much and no matter how old I was I still liked my kiss and cuddle. I would sit on his knee and he would say 'Your Dad is not very well, I think I will be dead soon'. I used to get all upset and say 'Please don't say that'.

'I'm sorry Hannah for the way I have been,' he would reply, 'it's just that I love you all.'

'I know Dad but your love is too possessive,' I would say.

'Do yourself a favour Hannah,' he would continue, 'do not bring children into this world because it's bad and will only get worse. He used to get upset when he spoke about his Mam and Dad, he really missed them.'

He told me why he never smoked; when he was growing up, he and his sisters would lock themselves in the toilet quivering in fear, hearing their parents argue over the last cigarette. We all nicknamed Dad 'Ashtray Harry', because if he came home and saw an ashtray empty or with a cigarette in it he would pick it up and throw it into the garden.

There was never a man who walked this earth who could match Dad for his smartness when he was dressed up. People would stop Mam and say, 'I saw William the other day Sally and he looked very smart'. When he would be getting ready Mam would double check there were no bits on the back of his jacket and that his trousers hung properly over his shoes and not on the floor, then she would hold up his overcoat for him to slip into, he never wore a normal tie - it 'had to be clip-on' he would say; if anyone grabbed your tie during a fight it would come off in their hand, allowing you to get the first punch in.

Some days we would listen to music, the likes of Frank Sinatra, Perry Como, Al Martino, Dean Martin but my favourite would have to be Mario Lanza, and to this day I have a plethora of all their music. Dad would always sing 'My Way' which used to bring a tear to my eyes. One day he was in the bath, Mam in the garden hanging out the washing, when a neighbour called over the fence, 'Morning Sally! What radio station do you listen to?' 'I don't,' Mam replied (thinking to herself we do not even own a radio). 'Who's that singing?

'Oh that's William he's in the bath… Can you hear?' Mam replied.

'Yes I can Sally, and what a brilliant voice.'

'Don't tell him that,' Mam said, 'you will make him big headed.'

I found out later in life that Dad used to sing in the pubs, and Mary had written to Hugh Green on Opportunity Knocks; he was accepted for audition but refused to go.

Mam and I were clearing a cupboard out on top of the stairs.

'Well I never,' Mam said.

'What is it?'

'Your dad,' Mam said, 'look years ago… He won the pools and he never even told me.'

There it was, a letter from Vernon's pools confirming he had won £500 pounds, a lot of money back then. To think what that could have done for the family, especially Mam.

Chapter Fifteen

Dad used to have a fish round, well he would buy the fish from the wholesalers and divide it into separate parcels, then I would help him deliver to the few customers he had who he charged two pounds, when that died down he and a friend would go to wholesale warehouses and buy anything from ladies tights to children toys, that seem to be going well and some of his customers used to place orders, they used to have goods on tick. A good seller were blankets, I nagged and nagged him until he let us have some, they kept us nice and warm.

Then eventually Mam had some towels and tea towels, Dad also had a friend who ran a catalogue. Poor Mam, anything she ordered she had to pay for herself, and if Dad wanted anything it was the same. Gradually Mam bought furniture, the first thing she ordered were single beds, what luxury; I used to sleep in the back room… William James and Edward in one room and Mam in another, Dad still preferred the sofa. I bought myself a combination wardrobe, I was so proud - it was white and with the few clothes I had I felt quite posh, what people took for granted every day, we never had.

In those days Men used to drive round knocking on people's doors selling whatever they had in their big white

vans... no questions asked, you just paid if you were inter-
ested. One week I was very lucky indeed, they knocked as
normal, for sale - a lovely pink bedroom carpet, on offer
for thirty-five pounds. William being a kind hearted young
man bought it for me. What luxury, apart from the front
room mine was the only other one with carpet.

Edward and I both worked at the same printing factory.
I was never really ambitious, but did once want to be a
hairdresser, but changed my mind and wanted to work in
a shoe shop. I enjoyed working at the factory, I would get
paid thirteen pounds fifty per week. If I worked overtime
I would get paid an extra fifty pence per hour. I saved up
twenty five pounds once, and bought Mam matching net
curtains for the house. Dad hated them, he used to say
people could see in.

The Telegram

December 1980 was very cold, we were forecasted a harsh
winter. After returning home one night after our company
Christmas party, I opened the door, Mam and Dad were
at home as usual, the sofa pulled towards the fire to keep
warm. I looked across to the fireplace, the wood on the top
was broken after Dad had put his fist through it on one of
his bad days. A white envelope was staring me in the face.
'Has Mary been in touch?' I asked, with that Dad jumped
up and slapped me across the face, 'You're drunk, get to bed,'
he shouted. I started crying, I had a feeling she was close.

The telegram, yes it arrived after Christmas, and the
words read: 'I thought you should know your daughter is
happily married to my son and they have two children Lucy,
three and Ronnie eight months.' Dad told Mam to reply
back to the woman and arrange for Mary to telephone Aunt
Rita's the following week.

I was present when the phone rang and Mam answered.

'Mary is that you? Are you alright? She said, 'then got upset. Dad took the phone off Mam and shouted, 'Mary!' a voice said. 'Hello Dad.'

'I'm not your fucking Dad, now put my daughter on the phone.'

Aunt Rita shouted out, 'William, do not swear down my phone!' Back then you shared a party line so you could be overheard.

I said hello to her, but Dad was angry… Looking back he had every reason to be, she walked out nearly nine years ago. After a while talking on the telephone it was agreed that Mary would visit in the February with the children, but not her husband.

The day had arrived and I was feeling nervous. The factory buzzer went off and it was time to go home. I looked at Edward and said 'What do we do?'

'Act normal,' was his reply, but Edward was not going home with me, he was married with a daughter and would visit a few days later.

I was going out that evening, so as normal, I started to get ready. As I walked through the door, Dad was sat on his own. 'You alright Dad?' I asked, I knew James, Mam and William had gone to Paragon station to meet Mary. He was just quiet. I used to sit on Dad's lap and say to him, 'I will never leave you.'

'That's what your sister used to say,' he would reply. Within an hour or so she would be walking through the door after all those years. I just kept praying under my breath he would not kick off.

I was washing my hair in the kitchen (it was too cold in the bathroom), we never had any heating, and with snow on the ground it felt even colder. All of a sudden the door opened, in walked James. 'Everything ok?' I asked.

'Oh Hannah,' he said. It was so emotional, Mam was

running towards Mary and she was running towards Mam, pushing Ronnie and Lucy running beside her.

Mam walked in next carrying Ronnie, with a smile which could light up the sky. I asked 'Where's William?' And Mam said, 'helping Mary with her bags and push chair.' As I turned to put the kettle on, in walked a dark haired woman with a little blonde girl. 'Are you Mary?' I asked.

'You must be Hannah,' she said. It felt strange looking at her, my sister, who I did not know.

Dad was six foot tall, with a fifty-two inch chest and a twenty one inch collar. He stood in front of the fire, Mary placed her hand on Lucy's back and gently pushed her forwards, 'Lucy say hello to your grandad William,' she said.

I went upstairs and not shortly afterwards Mary came up, 'Are you going out tonight Hannah?' she asked. 'Yes I replied, with my boyfriend.'

'Shush Dad will hear you,' Mary said. I looked at her, 'he knows I've got a boyfriend, he knows his parents... she seemed bewildered.

When I returned home that evening I felt something was not quite right. Mam was in the kitchen. 'What's wrong?' I asked her.

'Oh Hannah, your dad was alright at first, then he started questioning Mary; why she left and had she already met the children's father when she went... Is that why she left? Mary got upset and said she was going back to the Isle of Man, but I calmed the situation down, so she has agreed to stay a bit longer as long as your dad does not get angry.'

The week seemed to go ok, except for the day Mary and the children were due to leave. I went into the side bedroom and looked out of the window and saw Dad crying. 'Please Mary don't leave me,' he said.

'I have to,' she replied. 'I have a new life.'

'You can live here,' he implored, 'you and the children.'

'No Dad,' she shook her head. 'I am married now. I have a life in the Isle of Man.'

I found it so emotional watching them, I just cried. Mary kept in contact with the family but a week was not enough to get to know her. After all I was a little girl playing with dolls when she left and now I was a woman.

Mam went to visit Mary on her own in the summer for two weeks and while she was away I arranged a nice surprise. I had the hallway decorated with embossed wallpaper, it had a slight pattern over it with white emulsion, all the paint work was glossed. Mam's face said it all upon her return. The good old catalogue; the next purchase Mam made was an Axeminster stair carpet that she paid for weekly.

Aunt Ethel would spend Christmas day as normal with Aunt Rita but return home in the evening. Upon leaving one year, she slipped over the front door step and twisted her ankle. Due to her unfortunate stumble she demanded more and more of Mam's time, because there was no one else to look after her. On one of Mam's visits, she was complaining that her leg was really painful. 'Been brought up in the Victorian times,' she said, she was reluctant at first for Mam to take a look. Mam could not believe her eyes, gangrene had set in, so Mam called for the doctor, he said she had the heart of an 18 year old, but suggested that she go into a nursing home, which she did.

Dad suggested Mam go and visit Mary for two weeks. Mam could hardly refuse, she had been so exhausted, and it would give her a chance to get to know Mary a bit more, so off she went. She was only away a few days, but had to come back because Aunt Ethel had passed away. Mam was so upset, she had cared for her for such a long time and yet had never got the chance to say goodbye.

Not long before she went into the home, Aunt Ethel called in the solicitor and told Mam she had made her the executor of her will, even though Dad was her nephew, she said 'He will gamble everything away'. Mam had to sort clearing out the bungalow. I could not believe what I saw; in her wardrobe, for every coat there was a matching hat and gloves, there was bedding all wrapped up that never been opened, and to think all that time we did not have any. All the contents went to a dealer. I bet he conned her, Mam opened up an old tea chest and inside wrapped up was nine hundred pounds, that was a lot of money back then. Mam had to make the funeral arrangements, and pay any outstanding monies to the home which she dealt with, and with the little bit of money Aunt Ethel had left Mam she bought herself a blue bedroom carpet, God bless Aunt Ethel.

Broke Mam's heart

The man I had been courting, what a mistake that was... I was in a night club down Analby Road, a club a decent young lady should never have entered, but I was intrigued, I had never been in such a place and knew if dad found out I would be in serious trouble. I went there with a girl who was a bit more street wise than me. While I was on the dancefloor, a girl kept on bumping into me, I would just say sorry, even though it was not my fault. By the end of the evening there were six girls and two men waiting outside for me, they gave me a right kicking. My whole face was battered and I had my ribs kicked by the men. I really did not understand why this was happening, but later found out that one of the girls thought I was the 'Hannah' her husband had left her for. The next morning when I woke, I was supposed to go to work, but ended up in Hull Royal Infirmary. Mam had been called for (as she had stayed the night at Nana Dora's - since granddad John had passed away Mam and Aunt Betty would take it turns to look after her). When my dad found out what club I had frequented, he went crazy. I really thought

I was going to get another hiding. He jumped off his chair with such force the chair lifted up. He drove me up and own Hessle Road saying 'If you recognise any of them,' to tell him. I'm happy to say I never. Dad always said 'If anyone hurts his kids' he would of go to prison for us basically, he would have paid them back for what they did to me.

Chapter Sixteen

Riding my bicycle on the way to the Post Office, I was passing the taxi office, when a voice shouted 'Hannah.' I turned around to see the controller waving his hands at me.

'What's up?' I said.

'Your dad, William, he's had an accident.'

'What do you mean, an accident?'

'The police have just called here, your dad had our number in his glasses case, and asked if we knew the family.'

'Oh my Lord,' I cried. 'Mam, I need to go to Mam.' But for some reason I went straight to James who lived in the village with his wife. As I banged on the door he opened, 'Why did you not just walk in? And why are you crying?' he said.

'It's Dad James, he's been in an accident .'

'Does Mam know?' he asked.

'No, I came straight here, there's a taxi waiting outside, come on lets go…'

On the way back home we saw Mam strolling along with her shopping bag. James quickly got out of the taxi.

'Why's Hannah crying? I hope you two have not been arguing,' Mam said.

'No Mam, it's Dad, he's had an accident.'

I watched as Mam collapsed into a garden of one of the houses which lined the street.

We travelled to the Hull Royal Infirmary within minutes. Edward had arrived and we were waiting for William, who had gone to identify Dad's vehicle.

When William arrived at the hospital, he was as white as a ghost. He told us by the state of the vehicle, 'It's a wonder your dad is still alive'. We found out later what had happened; Dad used to visit a friend who had a motorway café, he drove out, looked both ways and went forwards, the next minute he was in a field, he blacked out and lost control of the vehicle, then the oncoming traffic crashed into him. The rescue team had to cut him out, the force of the impact threw Dad onto the back seat, and the engine landed ontop of his chest, the police said if it wasn't for Dad's large build, he would not be alive.

Whilst Dad was in hospital, he was diagnosed with diabetes, that was the reason for the blackout. Upon his discharge he was given tablets and a diet sheet, Dad's problem was sugar, he loved it. Mam would make him a cup of tea without sugar, but as soon as she turned away he would put six spoon fulls in. He also liked custard slice biscuits; anything sweet.

One Saturday, I was at my boyfriend's. He lived within walking distance of the town, so we went shopping, returning at around 3pm, his mother greeted us at the door, 'Hello Hannah, your Dad has been looking for you, he wants you home straight away. I think you better go,' she said. He was not in a good mood. 'Hannah,' she continued, 'I do not want any trouble, I have known William a long time.'

When I got home Mam and James were sat in the front room.

'Dad's looking for you,' James said.

'Mam what have I done?'

'He's found your pill,' she said. 'Oh no,' I panicked. 'Did you explain to him Mam?'

'I tried to,' she said, shaking her head.

I quickly went upstairs and brought down a suit case.

'Don't take that it's your Dad's,' Mam said.

All of a sudden the back door opened, he was so angry, in his hand was the garden pitch fork. He ran at me, and with that James jumped in front and said, 'You put it through her you have to put it through me first.'

Dad told James to 'Get out the fucking way.' He was shouting, 'How fucking embarrassing,' the electrician found them and gave them to me. That day we were having the house rewired and the man had to move the wardrobe. He picked up the packet and handed it to Dad, eventually when he calmed down Mam explained I had them for medical reasons, that made him more angry, to think that mam knew.

With James and Edward now married, I had to get away… but did not want to leave like Mary. I was twenty two years old. Friends my age were either living with someone or married. In Dad's eyes there was no one good enough for me. I applied for a nanny job in London and went for the interview… Edward said 'He won't let you leave.' I agreed, if Dad had said I could not go, then I would have done what I was told.

On January fourth, with my suitcase packed, and snow on the ground, my train was due to leave in four hours. That same day, Mam was taking delivery of an automatic washing machine; the old one had broken and it was costing fifteen pounds a week at the launderette. This was too much money, and too tiring for Mam, she would be there for two hours, sometimes I would take it for her.

There was a knock on the door.

'Mam,' I shouted, 'can you get the door please? I am in the bath.'

Mam never heard me, I put on my dressing gown and wrapped a towel around my head. I knew Dad had taken Sherry for a walk, so I would be alright answering the door.

As I opened it a man stood there, 'Morning love,' he said. 'I've got a washing machine for you.'

'Thank you,' I replied. 'Can you take it round the back please?' I replied, then shut the door.

All of a sudden I heard a voice say, 'That's my daughter you're talking about, shut your fucking mouth, you bastard'. The man walked back to the lorry and said to the driver, 'Core you want to see the bit of stuff that answered the door.' With the passenger door of the lorry open, no one saw Dad walking up behind. He put Sherry away, then had a right go at me and told me off for not being dressed properly. He soon calmed down, because he knew I would be leaving for London. He gave me a talk before I left, 'You must call every night at six o'clock, I do not want you getting involved in drugs or mixing with the wrong crowd and getting pregnant. If you do, I will cut you right up the middle.' They were very harsh words but they put me in good stead.

Mam wanted to come to the station with me, but I said no; it would be too upsetting for us both. Dad said he would take the dogs to the top of the street where the old train lines used to be, and watch the train go by.

'Good bye Mam, I will be alright, and I will see you at Easter, I shall come home every bank holiday, summer and Christmas, and I will earn some money and promise, you will never go without again… I love you. Bye Dad,' I turned to him, 'see you soon. I will call tonight.'

'How much money have you got?' he asked. 'Beside my train ticket I have eight pounds,' I replied. Here, Dad said, there's one hundred pounds, take it. I was shocked, 'No,' I said. 'I want to prove to you I can do this on my own. I have to go,' the taxi was blowing its horn. I got in the car and left. As I boarded the train I had very mixed feelings; I did not want to leave Mam or Dad, but I had to try and make a life for myself, plus I had been made redundant and jobs were sparse in Hull. As we pulled out of the station, the tears were falling down my cheeks, going alongside the Humber Estuary, as the train approached the old waste land, I saw Dad, he was stood waving. I called that night as promised and told him I had seen him.

Chapter Seventeen

When I first went to London, I found it really hard being away from the family, but I knew I had to make it work. I never really planned to stay for ever, but of course I met George and besides my family he is the best thing that ever happened to me. Edward had a son and daughter, as did James. William just had the one daughter, then in later years had another. Living in Hull I saw more of Edward's eldest daughter and son, because they were always at Mam and Dad's. Whenever I was home I would take presents for all my nieces and nephews, but it was always Edward's children I saw first. I have so many happy memories of them, they would get so excited knowing Aunty Hannah was coming home. I used to want to spend my time with Mam and Dad alone, but knew one of them would be there. I remember one day Mam and I took them both to Bridlington; we had such a lovely day, from leaving the house to returning home (Oh how I wish I could turn back time, even just for one day).

They were enjoying themselves so much, it was not easy to get them to the station for the return journey. At the time (Bread, the comedy was broadcast on BBC 1) I was walking back to the train station, my nephew was sulking, when all of a sudden he shouted out, 'She is a tart.' He was only nine years old, well Mam and I did laugh, because as he shouted it there were workmen on the roads and they heard him say it. (Of course it was a saying from Bread), I have photographs of the day which I treasure.

A few years later, another daughter was born into Edward's household. Oh bless, what a pretty baby and a right chatter box (just Like Aunty Hannah), she must have only been four years old when Mam and I took her to Withernsea, Mam smiling, so beautiful, as she watched her play on the beach in her little navy dress (and, as I used to call it the straw hat). She was no bother at all, until she wanted to go on a children's spinning wheel and wanted me to go with her. I'm surprised I got in the carriage, but I was not going to let her down.

A long day on a beach can make anybody tired but not her, she thought she would sleep on the bus all the way home, but oh no, she was 'chat chat chat.' We eventually arrived at the last bustop, hand in hand… as we walked down the street reminiscing on what a lovely day we had had, she was still chatting, then Mam turned and said 'Darling, just a minute, let me talk to Aunty Hannah.' She looked at us and carried on talking. I'm ashamed to say with all the laughter I just stood and peed myself. The way she looked me up and down it was funny. As soon as we walk through the door she said 'Grandad, Aunty Hannah peed herself.'

'Mucky sod,' Dad replied.

Chapter Eighteen

Easter weekend and I was back with the family. I had only been away twelve weeks, but it felt like a lifetime. Of course Dad wanted to know everything, and said 'Don't forget, if you ever need me, I will be there.' At first it was easy returning back to London but over the years my heart used to break leaving them behind. Dad used to go into a mood. Mam would say 'Oh, you can tell Hannah's going back to London.'

One day, after much thought, I decided I no longer wanted to be a nanny. I got employment working in an office, it was lots more money. On my home visit I would always make sure that Mam's cupboards were full of food, even down to cleaning products, especially toilet roll.

Dad would say 'Save your money,' but I could not bear the thought of Mam going without and me not being there. I used to send money home every month in a blue registered envelope to Hillary and Bill's and ask them to look after it for me till I got home at Christmas. They did, and each time I was home Bill would get the envelopes out and show me that they were all there and had not been opened. He used to say, 'Even my own children do not know we look after them for you.'

Christmas changed for the better. I used to make sure Mam and Dad had nice presents. I even hung up two stockings for them. I wanted one of those radio alarm clocks to take back to London, William made sure I had one but Dad was still not forthcoming with his money (however he did give me money to buy Mam a pair of boots every year). He was still gambling, but if he lost he would not rant and rave anymore, he would say 'I'm going to bed,' and later when he woke up he seemed much calmer.

Over the years I continued to work in London, and even though I was missing my family, I knew if I wanted to make anything of my life it was the best thing to do. I kept my word and called every night, but one night I was that tired after a busy day at work, I went home and collapsed on the bed. I did not wake till the next morning. The following night, when I called Mam said, 'Thank goodness you called.' I asked what was wrong. 'You did not call last night,' she said, 'and Dad told me to get a suitcase ready, he was going to London.' I explained to Mam that I was tired and had just fallen asleep. The last thing I wanted was Dad coming to me with his foul temper, even though I loved him.

Lucky Escape

I was about twenty five years old and did not really go out, but one night I did and I met a man. We started dating for a while and things went along smoothly. Then one night he showed another side of him… Whenever we went out to the pub and someone spoke to me he would accuse me of having an affair, he would tell me to sit at the bar and not look round; how foolish I was looking back. He then started to raise his fist and like Mam I thought I could not break away, till one day he hurt me so much I took an overdose. My father found out and travelled to London with William. When he arrived he was like a raging bull, he told my ex partner's family to take him to him because he was going to kill him, but all William wanted to do was get me back home to Hull. Even before we reached the M1 Dad kept asking me, 'Hannah come on, take me to him, you must know where he his'. We finally arrived home, Mam, she was so upset. 'Oh Hannah, look at you. I did not give birth to you so you could be a punch bag,' she said. It was then I realised what could have been. I wanted to stay in Hull, but to my surprise Dad said 'Hannah go back and make a life for yourself,' and I have done just that. With George to date, we have been together twenty four years and married twenty three, we both work hard, George more so, he does not gamble, he does not drink, only the odd one at home and to think… my life could have been so very different without him.

Working away at my desk one day, my colleague shouted, 'Hannah your Mam's on the line.'

'Ok please put her through,' I replied.

'Hello Mam, are you alright?' I asked. 'Why are you crying?'

'Oh Hannah, your Dad, he will kill me.'

'What's up?'

'I have spent this week's money in the bandit machines and I have no money left for food,' she said. 'I am at your uncle Bob's…' (Aunt Joan had passed away a few years earlier). 'He said he will give me the money if you can help out.'

'Of course I will Mam, put him on the phone.'

'Uncle Bob, please can you give Mam seventy pounds,' I said and I will put a cheque in the post for you straight away.'

'Hannah,' he said. 'I cannot believe what she has done, it's not like her.'

'I know Uncle Bob, please just give her the money. I am grateful, if Dad finds out, you know what he's like.' Mam came back on the phone. 'Why Mam? Why did you gamble your money?' You hate gambling. 'I know,' she said, 'but I just had one go, and won, so I had another go… but before

I knew it I lost all the money, so I panicked and went to see Uncle Bob.'

'Please promise me Mam you will never do it again,' I said, 'and if you need anything you let me know. I do not want Dad having a go at you.'

One night I received a call from Dad, he had lost some money and needed to let off a bit of steam, so I listened. I told him that I would come back to Hull and live there. He said 'Hannah, you make a life for yourself and don't forget to put your money in the bank.' He had a saying 'never tell your right hand what your left hand is doing.' By the end of the conversation he had calmed down. He was always giving out good advice, but would never take any, he always knew best. Aunt Joan once told me Dad used to carry hundreds of pounds in his trouser pockets, but gambling took over, we could have lived in a big house and had everything, especially if he had made it as a singer.

Diabetes is a terrible disease; it slowly damages your internal organs. Dad was prescribed a lot of medication. One day he accidentally knocked his foot, the toe nail broke off and started to bleed. Over time the foot got infected, then gangrene set in. He was admitted to Hull Royal Infirmary. I came home from London straight away… I asked the nurse about the gangrene, she replied 'it's the smoking,' (under different circumstances I would have started laughing). I told the nurse, 'Dad has never smoked in his life, he hates it.'

Mary came home, we all went to the hospital, standing at the bus stop on a freezing cold night, Mary very abruptly told me not to cry, as I am upsetting Mam.

'What did she know? She hardly knew any of us. But I kept the peace because of Mam. When we arrived the nurse told Mam that Dad's toe's would have to be amputated; the flesh was rotten. Dad was ok about it, but then he lost half his foot and that really hurt him, well you can imagine being a size 12 in shoe… he was in hospital for twelve weeks because his blood sugars were too high, they needed to be normal before he could be discharged. What furniture we had needed to be moved around for the fear of Dad bumping into it. I think he felt restricted as he could not jump up and go out like he used to… One sunny day he decided to sit in the garden, but first went to the kennel to let out one of the bitches, she was that excited to see him, she jumped up and knocked Dad clean over. He was so angry he got up and punched the dog in the face, she cowered away from him, yelping. Five minutes later he calmed down and stroked her, kissed her face and said sorry, he really loved his dogs. Mam used to say 'You think more of them then me.'

Whenever he went out for a drink he'd wear Hush Puppy shoes, but now with half a foot missing the hospital arranged for him to have a special pair of shoes. They were plain black with laces, very cheap looking, Dad hated them. Mam took Dad's Hush Puppies to some place in Hull city centre and they adjusted them. Eventually he was back to normal, going out drinking and gambling.

Sat in the front room, listening to Dad go on about money and 'What does Mam spend it on?' he always thought she blew it at bingo. 'William,' she used to say, 'the price of everything is going up, you go to the shops and find out for yourself.'

I have made a list Mam said, 'so off he went to the post office first, then onto the shops carrying Mam's shopping bag.' We both watched him walk by the window, we did giggle to ourselves. 'Mam, Dad's back,' I shouted. He walked in through the front door. I could smell the cold on him. 'The robbing bastards' he said. 'I don't know how people survive.'

'I told you,' Mam said, 'but you would not believe me.' Oh we did laugh.

Dad popped into the village supermarket, he stood patiently at the fish counter when all of a sudden a man pushed in front of him. Dad looked across at him, 'Excuse me,' he said. 'I was next.'

The man got all cocky, looking at Dad and grinning, thinking 'he's too old.'

Dad's blood pressure went through the roof, he punched the man so hard (in the middle of the floor stood a display of baked beans). The man's body landed on top of them. He walked out of the supermarket as calm as anything, then he came home and said to Mam, 'I am taking the dogs for a walk, the police may call… tell them I won't be long.'

'William,' Mam shouted, 'what have you done now?' Luckily the police never came.

Over the years Dad went out less and less. Mam would meet Aunt Betty on a Tuesday and have the afternoon at bingo, it was a release for her. I would phone if not once a day, three times. James ended up getting divorce and was living back home, he would help clean out the kennels and take the dogs for a walk and put Dad's bets on, as he still liked a flutter on the horses.

When I was home on holiday, I would notice a difference in Dad, he seemed to be losing weight and his skin looked a bit yellow, his hair was whiter, he was getting old. It used to break my heart to leave, I really wanted to go home. I had made enough money and always said I would like to open a café, there was no jobs in Hull, but people still had money to eat. I also wanted to buy the family home from the council, neither of them happened and I live with regret, especially about the home I grew up in.

For Mam's 60th birthday, I knew that Dad would not take her out, so I wanted to arrange something special. I contacted my brothers and suggested we took Mam out for a meal. I would come home and go straight to Edward's and James would then take Mam to bingo as a treat. Everything went according to plan, James got ready and put a suit on, Mam said 'You're a bit dressed up for bingo, son.' When they got off the bus, James made an excuse that he needed the toilet, so he asked Mam to wait in the station café. I was on cue, and when I saw him go back into the café, I was right behind, 'Happy Birthday, Mam,' I said.

'Oh Hannah, what a surprise…'

'You didn't think I would not be here for your 60th,' I replied.

'Oh look,' she said, 'there's our Edward.

'I know Mam, I went straight to his house when I got off the train. We all wanted to surprise you and take you out for a meal.'

We had a really nice evening, Mam had always wanted a gold bracelet, so I bought her one, she was so happy. It must have been about a year later, I was home on one of my breaks and I asked Mam where it was, she said 'Oh I lost it.' I said 'Please Mam tell me the truth.'

'Oh I pawned it,' she said.

'What? Why?' I asked.

'I had no money,' she said.

'Why did you not call me if you needed money?' I said. 'Come on, let's go and get it back.'

'It's too late,' Mam said. 'It was a long time ago… I did not have the money to get it back so I lost it. I was so upset to think Mam had to pawn it for a bit of money.

Chapter Nineteen

My family kept a lot from me with regards to my Dad's health. Mam looked after him with all her heart, she would make sure he had his medication, and when he went into hospital to have cataracts removed (he could not give me away at my wedding because he had gone 95% blind) Mam was there day and night, but Dad would say 'Get a taxi home Sally, I do not want you standing at the bus stop with all them drunks'. He used to make us laugh, he would not eat hospital food, Mam would take him sandwiches and pork pies and she was on the look out in case any of the nurses saw him.

Back home a single bed was placed in the front room for Dad to sleep on, he had trouble   walking the stairs and when he needed the bathroom Mam had to help him up and down again… He was a large man, but you never heard Mam complain. My brothers offered to help him bathe, but he only ever wanted Mam. He would say 'I am sorry Sally, you should not have to do this for me… Mam would say it's alright, I am your wife…' He would go onto say, 'I am sorry for what I put you through. I do love you Sally, that's why I married you.'

Dad was back and forth to the hospital for check-ups, but eventually he was to be admitted. His kidneys were starting to fail, but he also had a heart attack. Every day I would call the hospital, but they would not tell me anything, even though I was his daughter, one nurse called Maggie told me to ask for her, and even told me when she would be on duty. She appreciated I lived far away and would keep me updated on his progress.

August 8th 1996: I knew Maggie would be on duty when I called the hospital and asked for an update on Dad's condition. She gave it to me without any hesitation. I asked if I should come home and she said 'I think it will be best'. I put the telephone down and went into panic mode, there was a tube strike across London and I had to get from Chiswick to Feltham, then Kings Cross to Hull. With haste I set off, I arrived in Hull and went straight to my Mam. A friend drove Mam and I to the hospital, Dad was so pleased to see me, and we managed to have a ten minute talk on our own, he told me to be strong and to look after Mam and not let the boys run rings around her (I knew what he meant). 'Dad you are not going anywhere, please don't talk like that,' I said. 'I love you.'

'Hannah, I love you too,' Dad said, he also told me he was sorry for the past.

August 15 1996: I was diagnosed with a blood disorder. I telephoned and asked Mam not to tell Dad. She said, 'Hannah the nurses have told me that if Dad ends up back in hospital and anything happens they will not revive him, they will let him go with dignity. I could not believe what I was hearing. I was admitted to Hammersmith Hospital on August 16th, but all I wanted was to be with Dad.

I purchased a ticket to Hull for the 26th September. Dad's birthday was the 19th. I had sent him Mario Lanza and Frank Sinatra CDs, also a cuddly toy wrapped in blue ribbon, the card read 'Each time you hold me you will get kisses and cuddles, love always Hannah.'

Sunday September 22nd: I called home and spoke with Mam, usually Dad knew it was me on the phone, he would shout out 'I love you Hannah, but this time he never. He was sat in his favourite chair… I asked Mam to put him on the phone, I was not going until I heard his voice. 'I love you Hannah,' he said. 'Hello Dad, I love you too.'

'Your Dad's not well,' he said. 'I won't be here for much longer…'

'Dad, I love you. I'm coming home on Thursday and I am going to give you lots of kisses and cuddles.' The next voice I heard was Mam, she had taken the phone from him, he was crying. Apparently James had called Mary and she had arrived on his birthday and stayed until the Sunday.

Tuesday September 24th: I was getting ready for work, I felt a bit sickly but put it down to my medication, all of a sudden the telephone rang, I turned and looked at the clock, it was 7.10am. 'Hannah,' it was Edward's voice I could hear, I went numb… I knew what he was going to say, 'Dad passed away this morning.' I went crazy I threw the phone on the bed. 'No,' I screamed I want my Dad, I picked the phone back up, 'Hannah I am with your Mam,' Hilary said. 'My Mam,' I need to be with her, I cried.

Opening the door I walked into the front room, Edward was sat on the sofa, Mam looked up and put both her arms out to me. 'Mam,' I cried. I was absolutely devastated, Edward tried to talk to me… I shouted 'I hate you,' and ran into the garden. James was sat on Dad's chair. 'Why didn't any of you tell me he was dying?'

'You would have come home and just sat crying in front of him,' James said, 'and we did not want that. He was scared…'

'But you told Mary… Of all the people, she got to see him. She walked out years ago, she hardly visited. I shall never forgive any of you,' I shouted… and to this day I live with the regret of not being able to say goodbye to dad.

Edward told me that each night before Dad went to sleep he would look at the cuddly toy and say 'goodnight Hannah.'

The funeral needed to be arranged. I tried my best to help Mam but to be honest I could not cope. Mam had an insurance policy (to Dad's dislike) he always use to say if anything happens to me don't go spending loads of money. Mam said 'James, would you go upstairs and bring down dad's tin?' (he obviously knew what mam meant). I could not believe my eyes, he counted out seven thousand pounds; Dad had won it on the horses ten days before he had passed away.

Mam stood halfway between the kitchen and front room. I asked if she was alright, she looked very tired and of course upset. 'I need to go to the bank,' she said. 'I need bread and drink for tomorrow.'

'Mam,' I looked up at her. 'I will go to the bank, George will pick up some drink and Mary can pop over to Sainsbury's and get the bread.'

'Who are you giving out your orders?' Mary said.

'I am just trying to help Mam,' I replied. Still Mary's lack of concern shone through.

The day of the service had arrived, we were all trying to keep it together. Mam was in the bedroom looking out of the window, she asked me to leave her alone, there was so much sadness in her face. After the service we all went back home, I suggested we pop to the pub, it might have sounded callous to some, but we needed to get out the house. Mary sat next to Mam, all she could say was 'They hate me don't they?' 'They don't hate you Mary they do not know you,' Mam replied, 'don't forget they all grew up together.' I personally believe she felt guilty.

Eight weeks went by and Mam was not coping. I arranged for her to come and stay with me our James and his daughter came as well. I have photographs of them both outside Buckingham palace and shopping down Oxford Street,

Christmas was just around the corner all the lights were up. I went home that Christmas, Edward and I wanted to try and make it special for Mam… I showered her with gifts, I always went over the top and I think the rest of the family thought I was showing off, but it was not like that at all; I had made a promise years before and kept to it. Edward and I also got together and bought Mam a microwave oven. We had our tears that day, but we got through it. I just had to make sure that from now on Mam was taken care of.

Mam started to become a bit lost with herself, not knowing what to do… After all they had been married forty seven years and that's a long time to be with someone. One day James came to see Mam and suggested she join a club for the over sixties, Mam clearly did not want to go, but James said 'Mam, try it and if you don't like it you do not have to go back and if for any reason you get upset I can pick you up'. Mam loved it, she went every Monday from 11am till 4.00pm. It was a mixed club, a lot of the people had lost their partners, Mam would play bingo, they would have raffles and a pianist would turn up some weeks for those who wanted to dance. They would all have fish and chips for their tea, but to be honest it was the company that Mam liked and she made some nice friends, eventually Aunt Betty would go with her.

Every year the club would go away for a week with East Yorkshire Tours, the first one Mam went on they travelled to Isle of Wight. 'Mam please call me when you get there,' I said. 'Oh stop worrying,' she replied, 'I will be fine.'

'I am not telling you what to do Mam,' I continued, 'it's just you have never been anywhere on your own before.'

It was about ten pm when she called me, 'Hi Hannah, we have only nicely arrived, the coach blew a tyre on the motorway, so we had to wait for another one to arrive. I felt sick with worry all week until I knew Mam was safe back in

Hull. She loved going away, her favourite place to visit was Llandudno in Wales.

I had been married since 1991 and Mam would come and stay with us, we would of course continue to spend Christmas with her. My husband George thought the world of my Mam and my Dad, and in return they thought the world of him, in fact Mam called him 'Son.' George plays golf and Dad would call and talk to him about Nick Faldo, Mam and Dad both knew George looked after me and was a good husband.

When George first met my parents I was embarrassed because we did not have much and when Dad passed away if mam needed anything he would never stop me buying it or interfere with anything I did for her.

One year we went home, I noticed a plaster on one of the knobs on the cooker, I asked Mam why it was there, she told me 'It's to remind me that the ring does not work what with my eyes being a bit bad'. When we got back home we popped into Curry's and bought her a new cooker, it was delivered from the distribution centre in Sheffield. On another occasion we bought Mam a fridge freezer. When I first started work I bought Mam and Dad a box standard white kitchen with a few extra units.

Bad news again... Mam had been diagnosed with diabetes; she had cataracts like Dad and had to have them removed, she was also diagnosed with Glaucoma. I wanted to take the strain off Mam's eyes, she only had a small television. I called Mary and asked her if she would like to go halves on a flat screen TV for Mam for Christmas, but she said no. I bought it anyway.

Mary never really visited maybe once every four years she would send Mam thirty pounds for Christmas and twenty pounds for her birthday, sometimes for Mother's Day, sometimes not. I could never understand how a daughter could stay away from the women who brought her into the world, especially her own mother. Mary's daughter and son never really visited either, there was one time her daughter went to see her Nana and in her own words she told me Mary, her own mother had said 'Why are you going all that way? (Now that is cruel thing to say).

Chapter Twenty

I would go to Hull at every opportunity I had, George would come with me, unless work got in the way but he never minded, he knew what family meant to me, especially my Mam. We loved going out together, I remember one day in particular we went to see Aunt Betty, I knew how to get there, but getting back to Mam's was another story. I got lost so I said 'I know Mam, let's follow that bus, it's going to Hull Station.' Round and round in circles we went and did not get home till nine o'clock, we did laugh though, (I think we wet ourselves).

Another time Mam came to London and we went to Madame Tussauds. As everyone knows they are all wax works, well thought they were. Just before you exit there is a ride you go on, and at the end a still camera takes a photograph; Mam did make me laugh, we were turning the corner when she saw a policeman jokingly put her fingers up, he wasn't a waxwork, he was real. Mam loved going places; we visited the Sherlock Holmes Museum, we also took her to see Il Divo in concert at Wembley Arena, that was very emotional as they sang 'My Way', Mam grasped both our hands, I knew she was thinking of Dad… We played it at his funeral, if anyone did it his way it was Dad.

Back home Mam would continue to go to Monday Club

and the Tuesday meet with Aunt Betty, I used to hear about what they got up to. Mam did not have much money, but I always said if you want to go away I will pay for you.

From about the age of seventy-five Mam's health really started to detoriorate, she was diagnosed with diverticulitis, a problem with her intestines; it's not very nice at all and is really painful. On one of my visits I decided to take my mother in law, I did mention beforehand to Mam that I would have to look out for her as she had never been to Hull before. Mam said, 'Hannah I don't mind I am not jealous, and anyway I like Pauline.'

We all got in my car and went to a shopping centre just outside York, with Mam being a diabetic I knew how important it was for her to have something to eat and drink, but at the same time Mam did not like any one fussing over her, not like some people. We went into a Costa Coffee, where I got Mam a drink and a chicken sandwich, she sat quietly and only had a couple of bites. I said 'Are you alright?' 'Yes Hannah,' she said, 'I am just a bit hot that's all. She had started to walk with a stick.

'Mam, I am just going to have a look in the sports shop,' I said.

'Ok,' Mam replied. 'I will sit here on this bench.'

'As long as you're sure Mam.'

'I will be fine,' she replied. I could see her from the shop, I was only in there a couple of minutes, when I saw Mam, she looked a bit pale… I went straight over to her, Mam are you alright? She never spoke, but I noticed she was leaning over to the left and her mouth had dropped a little bit, I shouted 'Please someone call an ambulance!' A lady ran out of a shop and said 'There is one on the way.' A man sat directly behind Mam, who had never said a word. I asked him to open my bag, which he did but I could not believe he did not offer me any further assistance. The ambulance came and they took Mam to York Hospital, my mother in law and I followed behind in the car. I must have gone through every red light there was, but that was my Mam in that ambulance, no one else's.

When we got there the doctors said that Mam was a bit dehydrated, it was a hot day and diabetic people find it hard to cope. I asked the doctor to transfer Mam to Hull Royal but he said he could not do that (I was not happy with the doctor), I knew something was not right.

Edward was living at home, by this time he too had gone through a divorce, I explained what had happened and he said he would keep an eye on her. Mam used to sit up all hours reading since Dad passed away. She loved authors like Catherine Cookson and Joan Jonken but her favourite was Valerie Woods (I too read her books today). Edward had noticed that Mam was reading less and she used to sit in her chair with her head tilted to one side and would rest on her arm each time. He would ask 'You alright Mam?' She would say 'Yes, I'm fine Mam,' she never complained about anything whatsoever.

Edward had his cases packed, ready to go to on holiday for two weeks. I went home to be with Mam (it was lovely to have more time together). Mam had an appointment to see the optomologist, I was pleased I could go with her. Whilst in the room the nurse said 'I will be scanning your eyes today', I thought it was just routine. When the scan was over with, we both took a seat in the waiting room. 'Sally Baxter' a nurse called. We walked into the consulting room.

'Hello Mrs. Baxter, how are you today?' The consultant asked. Mam sat in the chair and the he started the examination.

'Do you drive Mrs. Baxter?'

'Not at my age,' Mam replied. 'Oh that's good, because I would have to arrange for your licence to be handed back.'

The next thing he said, 'I am so sorry Mrs. Baxter, I am going to register you blind.'

'That's ok,' Mam replied. I just got up and walked out of the room, I sat sobbing. When I re-entered the nurse asked if I was ok, I shook my head, I was devastated yet Mam the brave lady she was did not cry at all. I told Mam I needed the toilet, 'You fibber Hannah I know you have been crying,' she said

We were told that someone from the HERIB (Hull East Riding Institute for the Blind) would be contacting Mam to arrange a home visit. I took Mam back to the car and once inside just wept, 'Oh Mam I'm so sorry,' I said.

'It's ok Hannah,' she replied.

'It's not Mam, why did you not tell Edward you could not see?'

'I can,' she replied.

'Mam you have just been told you are blind, all that time you sat in the chair with your head rested on your hand, did you have a headache?'

'No, not really,' she replied.

'Mam, why did you not tell Edward, he would have taken you to the hospital. I just cried… 'Mam, please tell me you can see me. I can't bear to think you will never see my face again.'

When I got home Edward was just about to leave for the airport.

'Well what did the consultant say at the hospital?' he asked. I was not going to tell him at first, I wanted to wait while he returned from holiday.

'Tell me,' he said.

'Mam's blind.'

The look on his face said it all.

'Mam, have you been getting headaches? Why did you not tell me? I have already asked,' I told Edward.

'Look, I am here, I will look after her… You go away and I will update you when you are back, someone from HERIB will be contacting us to arrange a home visit. Mam never complained at all, yet my head was spinning with the worry of how she would cope. Mam still had to put eye drops in both eyes, but the right eye was like paper mash. (Writing this is tearing my heart apart), all Mam's reading had stopped, she had a talking book but did not like it. No more Monday club or holidays (I had offered to go with her if she still wanted to go away with her friends), no more meeting with Aunt Betty on a Tuesday, her life changed. She would just sit in a chair in front of the television. Mam said she could see outlines, but if Emmerdale or Coronation Street was on, or any of her favourite programmes, as soon as she heard their voice she would know who it was.

Edward really looked after Mam as I lived away. I had spoken to Mam about coming home to help Edward; one month in Hull and one in London, but she would have none of it, she was always saying 'It's not fair on George'. Each year Edward would go on his holiday and I would travel home to Hull to look after her, or she would stay with me. We would have a nice time; I bought her a wheelchair so it would be easy for Edward if she wanted to go out. We would have a laugh, Mam would say 'Strap me in… I used to say 'You're not a baby.' 'I know,' she would say, 'but I do not like going down the curb, I am always frightened I will fall out.' So from that day I would say 'Going down', Mam would laugh her little head off.

Mam's 80th Birthday: I wanted to do something special, so I called around the family and started to arrange a surprise party, but unfortunately due to one family member interfering too much it never came off. I even wrote to Daybreak TV and asked them if they could design a touch and smell garden, but nothing became of it.

Still determined to do something special for Mam, I arranged for flowers to be delivered, not just one bunch, but lots and a balloon. Her birthday fell on the Saturday, and Mother's Day was on the Sunday. I placed a notice in the Hull Daily Mail and then travelled to be with her. Mam meant the world to me, and I would do anything for her. One of her Grandaughters had a cake, that made Mam's day feel really special.

Summer 2010: I was working away at my desk, I thought I would give Mam a quick call, but she was in bed feeling under the weather… The doctor had been called and he told Edward Mam had an water infection. I asked him to keep me informed, this was on the Tuesday. Friday morning Edward called me at work, 'Hannah, Mam is still in bed,' he said. I told him I would be home in the morning. Saturday I set off at seven am, George told me to drive carefully as I had never driven all that way before, especially not on my own. I don't know how I got there but I did at 10.30am.

I walked into the bedroom, Mam had not been eating. I helped her out of bed and into the bathroom, then with mam all freshened up I asked her to come and sit downstairs, she refused at first, but I knew she needed to eat and eventually she agreed. Within half hour Mam had a cup of tea and something to eat. I stepped out into the garden to call George on my mobile when the back door opened and my nephew Joe shouted, 'Hannah, help… Nana.'

I ran into the house and dialled 999, Mam started to be sick. I went in the ambulance with her, I really thought she was going to leave me. It turned out she had septicaemia (the doctor should have called an ambulance on Tuesday). Mam was sent an appointment to attend a clinic on Newlands Avenue. James accompanied her and the doctor arranged for her to have a CT scan. The scan showed up Mam had had a stroke without even knowing it. It could have been before I was born, when I look back at everything Mam went through in the early years with Dad, it could have been then. Every time I telephoned home Mam would always say she was fine and not to worry about anything, and if I need you I will call (I loved her so very much). Remembering the time I took my friend Lorraine home with me, when leaving to return to London I would kiss and cuddle Mam on the doorstep, also cry my eyes out. As we pulled away from the house, Lorraine said 'Your Mother just said to me I don't know what Hannah will do if anything happens to me.' With that I turned the car around and went straight back, crying I asked Mam, 'Why she had said it? And was there something she was not telling me?'

September 2011, Edward was due to go on holiday, a friend of myself and George had very kindly offered to go and pick up Mam and bring her back to London to stay for one week. The second week my cousin Matthew was to look after her. I noticed a difference in Mam and it concerned me greatly, I kept on asking her if she was alright but as always Mam never complained… George had already agreed to sleep in the spare room, so Mam was close to me and if she needed the bathroom in the middle of the night I was on hand.

Mam had brought her wheelchair with her, so it was easy for me to take her out. I did though get upset to think Mam could not see, and only hear my voice. One day, after visiting George's Mam, we had just nicely got home and Mam needed the loo… I took her into the bathroom but always waited outside to give her privacy. Mam called to me, I noticed blood in the toilet… I gently explained, 'Mam please do not panic but there is a little blood, are you in pain?' 'No,' she replied. Over the week I kept a very close eye on her but also sent a text to Edward and explained. I also called Matthew and asked him to make an appointment with the doctor upon her return.

Chapter Twenty-One

Mother to Daughter

One afternoon Mam and I sat in the conservatory having a chat when she just came out with, 'You know I want to be buried with my Mam and Dad and not cremated,' she said. 'I replied 'Please, don't say that... Are you alright?'... 'Yes,' she replied.

I asked Mam if she missed Dad... 'Not anymore,' she said.

'What do you mean Mam?'

'Hannah when your Dad first passed away I did, but as the years have gone past it gets easier.'

'Who's Colin?' I then went on to ask.

'Who told you about Colin?'

'Edward did, years ago,' I replied, 'we were arguing and he told me I would not be here if Colin was alive.

'Hannah, when I first met your dad and we got married I was pregnant. I had a little boy and called him Colin but he only lived a couple of weeks.'

'Why?' I asked.

'He got pneumonia. and there was not the medicine then as today.'

'Where is he buried Mam?'

'Hannah there were no baby graves in them days,' she said. I did not ask any more, I could not bare to upset her.

'When I first met your dad he was very handsome,' she continued, 'all the girls liked him. Whenever we went anywhere he would talk to girls.'

'Were you jealous Mam?' I asked.

'No,' she said, 'but your dad was. I remember we went out dancing and we sat at a table when this man kept on staring at me your dad nearly bashed him up, it turned out he was admiring my teeth.'

'Why does Aunt Betty not like Dad? I asked.

'Because he hit your Uncle Ron,' she said. 'Hannah I left your dad once and went back to Nana and grandad.'

'Why?'

'Because of his bad temper and verbal abuse.'

'Why did you go back Mam?'

'Because Mary would not stop crying…' She missed him. I am glad you did Mam, because I would not have been born.

Hannah, your dad and I went to a dance hall once and I was presented with a bouquet of flowers, your dad's jealously took over and he pulled the heads off them.

Two policemen came once to your Nana's and arrested your dad, they put him in handcuffs with an officer either side of him… As they were getting into the car, the man who used to live across the road came out of his house and shouted something at your dad, your dad actually pulled both officers together and then nutted the man.

"Did you go out much together?'

'No, he never took me anywhere, he used to say women should not be allowed in pubs. However there is one thing I shall say about your dad, he never drank or played cards in the house.'

'I can't believe how much you suffered Mam.'

'Oh that's nothing Hannah, I came home from shopping one day to find he had taken up the stair carpet and flogged it to go gambling.'

'Oh Mam.

'He was always selling my furniture…'

'Is that why we never had much when we were kids? I do not blame you Mam.'

'Your dad would never give me any money Hannah, and if he did I had to pay him back.'

'I loved him Mam, he was my dad.'

'But I don't like to think what he put you through Hannah, you were a daddy's girl. When he worked nights on the docks he would come home in the morning and get into bed, you would put your arms out to him. Your dad would say 'wait a minute get in bed,' put a sheet over him, then wrap you up. When you were first born he took you in his arms and sang 'Because God Made Thee Mine'.

'I know Mam, you told me that before… that's why I had it played at my wedding.'

'Mam,' I asked, 'why did Mary leave home?'

'Because your dad was too strict with her, he was with me too and I never left. Hannah you could have anything, if I told you off you, you would always run to your dad.'

'What I do not understand is how a daughter could stay away from her Mam for all those years,' I said. 'You went through hell and as I remember it, she could have at least tried to contact you.'

'I think she blames me for not leaving your dad.'

'Mam you have nothing to be blamed for, you went back to him because you missed him, and maybe, just maybe if she had stuck around things might have been different… I know he was strict and I respected him for that Mam, he put me on the straight and narrow.'

'Your dad was a lot of things,' she said, 'but he loved his kids.'

'I get fed up Mam with the rest of them saying, 'You were only a baby.'

'I remember a lot, take no notice of them Hannah.'

'Do you love me Mam?'

'I love you more than anything Hannah,' she said.

'I love you too Mam, with all my heart and you know whatever you need I will get it for you.'

'I wished I had a baby sister or brother younger than me Mam.'

'Hannah you know when I had my hysterectomy,' she said, 'I was also carrying a baby but I had cancer so they had to take the baby away.'

'Was that the reason for your breakdown Mam?'

'Yes,' she said, 'and everything else… I just could not take anymore.'

'After everything he put you through, did you love him Mam? I don't mind you telling me the truth.'

'Yes I did… Once Hannah your dad was one of the nicest men you could meet, when he had money in his pocket he was always smartly dressed when he went out and very handsome but after he had been in prison, he changed.'

'Why did he go to prison Mam?'

'For handling stolen goods, or fighting… The police tapped into our house phone.'

'Is that why we never had one until I went to London?'

'You where the apple of your dad's eye's Hannah,' she continued, 'and I think you loved him more than me.'

'No Mam that's not true, I have always loved you the same. You are my world Mam promise you won't ever leave me.'

'No,' she smiled, 'of course not.'

Chapter Twenty-Two

Edward had returned from holiday and Mam was taken into hospital for some tests. I went home to be with her. On the day Mam was discharged I went to collect her. She had a room to herself.

'Hi Mam,' I said.

'Hello Hannah,' she replied, 'are you alright?'

'Yes I am, just waiting for my hospital notes and medication… Did everything go ok Mam?'

'Yes, fine' she replied, and with that a nurse walked into the room and Mam said 'I have just been telling my daughter they are not cutting me open, not at my age.'

I asked the nurse why Mam had said that, but she just replied I cannot comment, your mam will need to see her GP in a week to ten days.

'But I need to know if there is anything wrong, I live far away,' I explained. On the way home I asked Mam was there something she was not telling me? 'No' she replied and the next day I returned to London.

One week later on Sunday, I was preparing lunch when my house phone rang.

'Hello Hannah?' Edward said, 'It's Mam, she's having a stroke, the ambulance is on its way. Georgie is here with me.' Georgie is Edward's eldest daughter. I went into panic mode, 'ok Edward I am on my way,' I said. I have never driven so quickly, George came with me because it was getting dark early, being November. George was in regular contact with Edward while I was trying to concentrate on driving to the hospital.

We arrived at Hull Royal infirmary at 11pm, Edward had stayed with Mam all day, so after an hour or so I told him to go home and rest, George went with him. I never left Mam's side until she was comfortably admitted onto a ward, while I was waiting, Edward's son Billy turned up.

Mary had been informed and came home, it was the first time in four years. I wanted to say a bit more than 'Hello how are you?' But all that mattered was Mam getting better. The week I was there I visited Mam every day. One day in particular stand out, I was in the kitchen, Edward and Mary were talking about the past, and as usual I was told - you were only a baby. I got upset and started to cry, I asked Mary for a cuddle, I was so afraid of losing Mam, Mary just abruptly told me, 'We all have to go one day, and mam is nearly 82.' Did she have no feelings at all?

On my way to the hospital I was popping into to town to buy Mam a new nightie and asked Mary if she would like me to get one from her, 'No, I will take Mam something later,' she replied. I was still upset, so told her not to go visit Mam as I wanted to be alone with her, as I was returning to London the next day.

When I arrived at the hospital Mam asked, 'Where is Mary?'

'At home,' I replied.

'Have you been arguing?'

'Yes.'

'Take no notice,' Mam said and cuddled me.

'You're my Mam,' I said, 'I love you.'

'I know Hannah I love you too.'

The time came for me to leave, I kept walking away, then going back on the ward and cuddling Mam, I spoke to the nurses and asked them to look after her.

When I arrived back at Mam's house Mary asked if everything was ok? And did Mam have any bananas? I don't know, bananas I thought, she has not seen her mam for four years and all she is worried about was if Mam had any bananas.

Chapter Twenty-Three

Eventually Mam was discharged and seemed to be getting along, she had a visit from the stroke association to see how she was progressing and to have a chat with Edward as he was her main carer. I telephoned everyday, if not twice.

December 2011, George and I decided to go away at Christmas, but beforehand I needed to see Mam. We travelled to Hull on Saturday the 3rd of December, she was so pleased to see us both, I will never forget, we had such a nice evening - Edward and George were joking with each other and Mam could not stop laughing.

Looking back we seemed to reminisce a lot, Mam sat in her usual place in front of the television, she seemed fine, I told her how much I loved her and that in between Christmas and New Year, once we returned from our holiday, we would be back to see her.

Unfortunately we had to travel back to London the next day, we were due to fly out from Gatwick on Monday 12th, the night before we stayed in a hotel. I called Edward to see how Mam was and he told me she was in bed. When I asked why, he told me 'She feels a bit cold.'

'Ok Edward, I will call you Tuesday,' I said, 'as we will be in the air tomorrow.'

We arrived in Egypt, but I could not settle, I kept saying to George, 'Mam will be alright won't she?'

'Yes,' he tried to reassure me.

Throughout the first week, I kept in contact, but one day the words I was dreading ripped my heart apart. Matthew answered the phone.

'I will not lie to you Hannah, Aunty has not got long.'

I just screamed and ran out the hotel. The staff at the resort were very helpful and got me a flight the next day.

5pm, Friday 23rd December, I arrived home, the majority of the family were already there. Aunty Betty was sat in the front room, she had been there all day.

'Hello Mam.'

'Oh Hannah, it's so good to see you, where is George?'

I winked at James, 'Mam, you never guess, he's had to go into work to fix a door, but he will be home soon, it's as if she knew she was dying.

I had to bite my lip to stop me from crying, my heart was broken. Seeing Mam lying there; she had lost about three stone in two weeks, I just wondered how could this be. I laid with her, holding her hand, never letting go, telling her how much I loved her. By Saturday she was fading fast, I let her know all the family loved her very much. I still regret saying what I said ('Mam I do not want you to leave, but if you have had enough it is ok, don't be scared'), I even sang to her.

Christmas day, 12.40 am, with my hand in hers, she took her last breath. I went numb all over, I walked downstairs and poured a Scotch, when the undertakers came to collect her I fell to pieces. Between Edward and I, we called around the family. I could not believe Mary, Mam had gone and all she could say was, 'I cannot get there with it being Christmas.' She did not even tell her daughter that her Nana had passed, till after Christmas. What was more important I thought opening a Christmas present. There would be plenty more

Christmas days, but not another beautiful mother.

I cried myself to sleep and woke at 6.30 pm on Christmas Day to the vision of Matthew stood at the side of the bed. All I wanted was my Mam, one day she was laid next to me and the next gone. George could not get to me for a few days, it was not that he was being callous he wanted to remember Mam how she was; George been very fond of her.

Mam's service took place on the 6th of January 2012. I carried the coffin, Mam brought me into the world and I would carry her out, my heart was breaking. During the service I read out the following.

"Such a Place, Mother"

Such a place holds no one,
Except for one so Dear.
Such a place can't be entered,
Within my heart, right here.

Such a place is held special,
And brims, with over flowing love.
Such a place can't be touched,
It's God's gift, from Heaven above.

Such a place can't be broken,
Nor battered, with life pains.
And this such a place, on its own
Will always, eternally reign.

Such a place even marriage,
Friendship and love, cannot take,
Such a place is locked and bound,
With chains, no man can break.

Such a place can't be lost,
Nor replaced, by no one, no other
Such a place in my heart,
Is held, just for my Mother.

I love you with all my heart.

Chapter Twenty-Four

Mary had managed to get home the day before, and went back the day after. George and I travelled back to London on the Sunday. I cried all the way home and remained there until February 14th… I had a breakdown, I had thought on more than one occasion about taking my own life, but I knew Mam would never forgive me.

I visit Hull on Mam's birthday and near Christmas, I still have family there, but it's not the same. I take the same route and drive past the old family home, both into Hull and out.

Looking back over the years I do not condone what my dad had done, he was my father but I think he must have suffered from some kind of Schizophrenia.

Since then I have found out what really happened to baby Colin, Dad was in one of his foul tempers and was arguing with Mam and punched her in the stomach. The reason Dad fought with Uncle Ron, was because when Mam returned to her parents with William and Mary, Dad went there, all angry, wanting Mam home. My Nana lifted up a poker and went to hit him but Uncle Ron got in the way and the fight broke out at the court hearing the judge told both side of the families they were not allowed to contact each other.

Looking back over my childhood years, both parents loved me, but I owe a lot to my Mam for the way she kept the family together, and for that I am eternally grateful. You suffered a lot of pain and I watched you slip away, yet my love for you grows stronger every day, there is not a day goes by that I don't think of you. I get through each day just remembering the love, not the bad. To my father I loved you, but through your possessive love you caused so much heartache and pain.

We never let go.

Chapter Twenty-Five

I am happily married to George, and still living in London. Edward has a new partner Lorraine. James also has a new partner, Sue, they have been together for twenty-five years. William is suffering ill health due to diabetes.

Mary is still living on the Isle of Man, I do not have a relationship with her, unfortunately I could not attend her son's wedding due to having an operation, and her husband called me to tell me she would never forgive me. I know it was harsh of me, but on the day of her son's wedding, I sent her a text and told her I would never forgive her for not seeing our mother.

February 13th 2013, working away at my desk, I received a call from William's son-in-law. William had been rushed into hospital, I collapsed on the floor and shouted 'Someone help me.'

Due to the extent of his diabetes, his kidneys had started to fail. I knew I could not drive all the way to Hull, so I telephoned George and he told me to get the train, as by the time he had got home from work it would be too late, and the weather was turning nasty, It had started to snow. Making my way to Kings Cross I did not even know if the trains would be running. Just before I boarded the train at

7pm, I made a call to my sister in–law, she had informed me that the whole family was there, and that Williams heart had given up, but the doctors resuscitated him and he fought hard to stay with us.

As I boarded the train the tears were flowing down my face, the evening was very cold and the further we travelled up North the worse the weather got. The journey seemed to take forever, I went to the cafe bar to get a coffee but to be honest I bought a Jack Daniels, the lady behind the counter asked me if I was ok, but when I told her the reason I was travelling she showed me so much compassion, and told me to stay with her and when we arrived in Hull she would take me to the hospital, her car was parked at Hull station. I arrived at Hull Royal Infirmary at 11pm, running through the door with my heavy bag, shouting 'Please someone help me, I need ward five. The security staff came to my aid and took my bag.

When I walked towards William's bed my heart sank, I really thought he was going to die. Ten minutes later Mary, her daughter and son arrived, they had travelled all the way from the Isle of Man, I had not seen her since the day before Mam's service and whatever my thoughts were, I had to keep them to myself. That night Mary went and stayed with Edward, I sent my sister in-law home for some rest, Edward took my case and I stayed at the hospital all night. Mary's son was the first to arrive the next morning and mentioned they would be travelling back home, but he wanted to take flowers to his Nana's resting place but Mary refused, she wanted to get back. Even then I thought to myself, still you think only of yourself, you could not be bothered to visit your Mam when she was alive, and how cruel not wanting to visit her resting place now. I also felt shocked that she wanted to return so soon. Her excuse was that she needed to get back to work, I kept quiet, even though I was full of anger. Yes I could understand her daughter and son returning, but our brother was still not through the worst.

The doctors explained to the remaining family that William would have to start dialysis. I stayed for two weeks, and visited every day. I was going nowhere until William was out of danger, I kept my employer updated and they were very supportive towards me. From that day forwards William really suffered, throughout 2013, he was back and forth in hospital not only that he had a hospital bed brought into the home and the nurses would visit just about every day administrating injections and constantly checking his blood levels and sugar. He also suffered with potassium levels, which is very dangerous when you are a diabetic. William was being supervised by a dietician and it was explained to his wife what he could and could not eat. William had to sleep wearing a mask, because if he did not the chances were he would stop breathing.

My sister-in-law did what she could, but to be honest a full time carer should have been there. Some days William's wife would get up at 4am and go and look after her grandsons while her eldest daughter went to work. Then by the time she got home she would be exhausted, not only as William needed round the clock care, but obviously because they could not sleep together, so in the middle of the night William would call out to her and she would rush downstairs, he would be in the middle of an hypnosis? If only Mam and Dad where here, I would constantly say to myself, but I knew it would break their heart.

There was one part of 2013 when it seemed William was making a break through, however in November 2013 he walked into the back garden, and unfortunately he stood on a rusty nail and it went through his left foot. An infection had set in which lead to him having three toes removed. He ended up back into hospital. I would call my sister-in-law every day to check on his progress and some days I would call the hospital and ask the nurses to tell him I had called and that I loved him. When we were growing up, all our siblings would have misunderstandings or cross words, but not William and I.

Eventually William came back home on the Friday, then Monday came and his wife popped to the local shops. Upon her return you had to walk through William's room to the kitchen, she called out his name, but he did not respond, right away she called an ambulance. When the paramedics turned up, they told her any longer and he would have died. He was admitted to hospital again, the doctors said due to the shock of him having his toes removed his heart had weakened. It was like reliving everything Dad had gone through, my heart used to ache at the thought of William lying there suffering, I felt so helpless.

Chapter Twenty-Six

March 2014, George and I travelled to Hull to place flowers down for Mam's birthday. We had already decided to spend as much time visiting William as possible, as I constantly worried about him. As we walked through the front door my heart sank, I could not believe that someone could live the way they did, it was the 21st century not the Victorian era. They had no money, no food. William sat there with a fleece blanket around him, which I had previously bought him. I went to the shops and picked them up bread and milk, luckily I had bought a few things before hand to give them. As we drove away George said 'It's heart-breaking to see them live the way they do, and we need to help,' (George has a very big heart). I knew the youngest who lived at home worked, but she didn't earn much money so we decided we would do what we could.

Material things are not as important as your health, but at least having the necessities could help. Before we visited the next day we went and bought paint and lampshades, then I took his wife out and bought her a couple of items for the kitchen. Once back in London we sent parcel after parcel, even arranging for a farmer in Scotland to deliver meat. I just could not get it out of my head, my brother suffering and his wife doing the best she could.

William's foot seemed to be healing, but his eyes had now started to deteriorate, one eye developed a cataracts and the other a bleed behind. He was due to have laser treatment on the 12th June but on the 11th I called as usual and my sister in-law informed me William had been complaining of stomach pains so she called an ambulance and he had been admitted to hospital. On Thursday morning I called and she told me he had pneumonia, and was on a drip with antibiotics flushing through his system. I was too upset to concentrate at work so I went home. I was very worried for him, not only because of how dangerous pneumonia is but because I knew (due to his other health problems) it could be life threatening.

Friday 13th, I went into to work, at 10.50 am I called home for an update on William. My sister in-law had told me she was just about to call me; she was on her way to the hospital. They had put William on dialysis and within a minute he had collapsed. I did not want to hear it; I just put the phone down. I called back a couple minutes later and told her 'I am on my way home,' I just wanted to be with William.

I went into panic mode; I had a bad feeling… My neighbour helped me pack a case, and just before I boarded the 1.48pm from Kings Cross to Hull (I was due to arrive at 4.20pm), I called my sister in-law… She went quiet.

'Please, no,' I said. 'Please do not tell me he has gone.'

'Hannah he died twice and they resuscitated him, but through this they have cracked one of his ribs and he only has two to three days to live.'

I just screamed, 'Oh, no.'

I boarded the train, it was getting rather congested and all I could hear was people complaining. I wanted to shout, 'Shut up!' But it was not their problem, what I was feeling inside. As soon as the train pulled away and the cafe bar opened I was there, Jack Daniels and coke in my hand. Drink is not the answer, but it kept me calm. Once I arrived in Hull I got a taxi straight to the hospital. As the taxi pulled into the car park I saw my sister in-law waiting for me. 'Hannah,' she said, 'please do not let William see you cry, he does not know… James has just left.'

It was mentioned later that James was told not to visit any more, he had said his goodbyes and the family knew he did not like hospitals, the main thing was he saw him, not like Mary.

I walked onto the ward and a nurse approached me, are you Hannah from London? Yes,' I replied. 'Is there somewhere I can put my case please?' She took me straight into her office where a nurse explained to me that William was at the end of his life. I just broke down; another nurse fetched me a cup of tea. I looked up and could see my sister in-law at William's bedside. I was feeling so much pain, so I could only imagine what she must have been going through.

Walking towards his bed, I said, 'Hello William it's Hannah.'

'Hello Hannah,' he said. I told him George was coming a couple of days later and next week the three of us were going to go out for a Guinness.

'I don't like Guinness,' he said. Within minutes Edward had arrived, he had been there every day. I stayed at the hospital till 9pm and told William I would be back the next day, but the nurses informed me that he was going home to die. What I could not understand? Apparently his wife and daughters wanted him home and the Macmillan nurse would be on hand.

'Has he got cancer,' I asked.

'No,' my sister-in-law said, but they have experience in this kind of situation.'

Before I left with Edward I told her, 'I will go straight to your home in the morning, if anything changes please call me straight away, even if it's the middle of the night, I shall get a taxi.'

As I arrived at Edward's home I felt numb, and did not know what to do or say, he told me Mary had been informed, but did not want to come home and say goodbye to him, she just wanted to remember him like Mam again. I wanted to speak out, but kept quiet, we both agreed we did not want him to go, but could no longer stand him suffering the way he had done for years. I think I said 'You would not let a dog suffer the way he has.'

We were all trying to come to terms with the fact that William was at the end of his life. The next day I arrived at William's and was told he would be home at tea time, so I went with his youngest daughter to the shops, because next day was father's day. As we walked into the card shop, I just walked straight back out. I could not bear to watch her choose a card, knowing anytime now her father would be taking his last breath.

Returning to the house I helped prepare for him to come home. A nurse arrived to discuss things with his wife and it was agreed I could stay there, then the call came through the hospital, I had forgot to order William's oxygen, and he could not come home without it. Eventually two ambulances and four paramedics brought William home at 11pm, which was disgusting. I could hear him crying, so I climbed into the ambulance the paramedics decided after an hour that they could not get him in the house; if he took two steps he could die and they did not want to take the responsibility. It was 1am when they took William back to the hospital and I went with him, there was no way he was staying on his own. We were put in the dialysis room and I pulled up a bed and slept next to him. He kept holding my hand and rubbing my thumb, he would cry 'Hannah I am not going home, am I?'

'Of course you are,' I would say holding back the tears. I kept thinking I wish Mam and Dad were here.

I needed the loo and told him, 'I won't be long.'

'Don't leave me,' he said.

'I'm not William,' I replied. 'I will be straight back.' He managed to get some sleep and woke at 2.35 am, he looked up at the ceiling and said 'Hiya.'

I asked him 'Who is it William?' And told him, 'it's father's day today'. He got upset and told me he misses his mam and dad, and did not like not seeing them. I told him 'they are here William, watching over you.' It was then I could feel the presence of them both and knew the time was drawing nearer. I remember lying next to him; I was on my right side. William placed his hand on the left side of my head and rubbed my hair, how he managed it I do not know, I just laid still for a few seconds. I think then he was telling me goodbye.

He asked me where his wife was and I told him 'She will be here in a couple of hours.'

He got upset again, I told him not to cry but I walked outside the room and just burst into tears. He went to sleep again till 6am and a nurse brought us both a drink. Again he asked for his wife.

'Two more hours, William and she will be here,' I said.

He told me he did not want his youngest daughter there, when I asked why he said 'because she gets too upset.'

Eventually his wife arrived and his youngest daughter, then Edward's and William's eldest daughters. He seemed in good spirits and was talking to us. I just kept telling him I loved him, I stayed till 2.30pm. I needed to have a bath and try to get some sleep, yet I did not want to leave him.

Edward and I left at the same time. I offered to get a taxi but Edward refused. On the bus home Edward told me to go home and said he would go to Sainsbury's to get us something for dinner. I did as I was told; when I walked through the door I made myself a cup of tea, then lit up a cigarette. Afterwards I took a bath, I came back down the stairs, you could hear a pin drop, but I said out loud 'I need to go to bed…' As I climbed in I placed my mobile next to me. I woke at 5.30pm and felt terrible.

My mobile rang at 7.30pm, it was William's eldest daughter asking me if I was going back to the hospital, but I told her I needed one day away to catch up on some sleep. I just could not sit at his bedside watching him die, she understood but fifteen minutes later Matthew turned up to see William, he called me afterwards and said William was just sleeping.

I awoke on Monday and rang my sister in-law to tell her I would meet her at the hospital, she told me she had rang and the nurse explained he had hypo in the middle of the night and they had given him a strong dose of morphine. I was the first one at the hospital that morning and William was sleeping. I wiped his mouth as he was losing fluid (I knew I had seen this with my Mam).

'Hello William, it's Hannah,' I said, but he never responded. Within ten minutes, his wife and youngest daughter arrived. I looked at her and shook my head, we whispered to each other we are staying all day and night. She called his name but he did not respond, then she gently tickled his chin, he opened his eyes and said 'Hiya,' then closed them. The nurse came to us and asked if we could leave the ward for about forty-five minutes while they gave the other patients their lunch. I did not approve of this, but once again kept quiet.

We all went to the family room but my sister in-law and I went outside for a cigarette, whilst outside her mobile rang, it was time, we could not wait for the lift… We both ran up five flights of stairs, I just kept saying 'Dear Lord, in the name of the father, please hear my prayers', the curtains were closed around his bed, his daughter was sat there. His eldest daughter had just pulled up in the car park, Edward had been contacted and he was running down the street to try and get to him.

I kissed William's face and kept telling him I loved him, and for one moment he looked like he had passed over but as soon as we said 'Edward is on his way,' he moved his mouth again, he was tired, he had had enough. Mam and Dad came for him. I said 'William don't be scared, it's ok to go,' tears ran down my face. This was not fair, he was a husband, father and grandfather, but he was my William and for fifty two years I had loved him, then he slipped away. No more suffering, no more pain, but I was left with the pain of never seeing him again, nor hearing his voice, but what I will always remember is when he told me 'Hannah I know I don't say it a lot, but I love you.'

After a while we went and sat in the family room, Edward walked through the door.

'How is he?' He looked at me.

I shook my head, 'he's gone,' I said.

No, he cried and ran to his bed, he was four minutes late. Before we left the hospital I went into a room where William was laid. I just placed my hands across his chest and kissed his lips 'I love you my William, I shall never forget you.' I cuddled him as though he was still breathing.

When Edward and I returned home he went crazy, he punch the living room door, he had watched my father being taken out of the family home by undertakers, he was also with me when Mam took her last breath, but he was only four minutes late to say goodbye to William. I have never seen Edward with so much pain in his eyes; he visited William every week, and lived so close to him. When Mam passed away, I knew he was hurting, but he did not show it, at least in front of me. In fact I have always been afraid about talking to him about Mam unless he mentioned something. First you see Dad always told us not to cry, but I think the loss of William seemed to bring out all his anger and emotions.

That evening Edward's daughter picked me up and I went to stay the night with her and her family. We talked about everything, how William had suffered with the loss of Mam and Dad. I explained to her that in a way I was relieved he had gone, because he suffered so much. We talked about when I was a little girl, and how much he loved me, and a smile came to me. It was William that bought me my first suitcase when I came to live in London.

The next day my niece dropped me off at the bus stop, she had to attend a meeting first thing. I could have stayed, but there was no point on my own. As I waited for the bus I glanced across the street and realised opposite was Greenwood Avenue where Nana Dora lived and Granddad John. Boarding the bus I sat right at the back, tears running down my face, I could feel people looking at me but did not care for them as I was suffering inside. As we pulled into Hull interchange my connecting bus had not arrived, I called my mother in- law, just talking and crying,

On the way home I was still nervous about going back to Edward's because of the previous night. I knew in my heart he would not hurt me, but I still needed to be careful of what I said. Arriving near Hessle I glanced out of the window. I saw the stop I used to get off to go to our family home, quickly I jumped off the bus and found myself walking through the streets I walked when I was growing up. As I turned the corner, there it was staring straight back at me, the old family home. Tom Jones, 'The Green Grass of Home' song came into my head and I started singing, all choked up. I turned to the right and knocked on an old neighbour's door, not knowing if they still lived there… The door opened and they took me in, 'sit down Hannah, we will make you a cup of tea,' they said.' How kind they were, Robert spoke to me while Sue made the tea. 'We are so sorry to hear William has passed away,' they continued, 'we often see Edward walk by.'

I explained to Robert that I wanted to knock on the old front door and see if the new residents would let me in. I felt it might give me some kind of closure.

'Hannah,' Robert said, 'you were always a very close family, I think it would not do you any good to just keep your memories you have inside you. If you go into the house the furniture will most probably be different, nothing will look the same.'

But I believed my Mam's spirit was still there, and I wanted to ask her to come with me. After a while, talking with Robert and Sue I felt a little calmer.

As I walked towards the home it seemed we were all still living there, Dad in front of the television, Mam in the kitchen, James and William at work, Edward relaxing after one of his boxing matches, me nagging for something and the dogs in the garden. For a few minutes I stopped at the end of the driveway, just staring. It was strange, the house had the same blinds up at the windows, even the same colour, looking at it hurt me even more, I waited hoping someone would come out of the house so I could speak with them.

Arriving back at Edward's I never mentioned anything about my morning events. He asked me if I was ok, 'yes' I replied. 'You?' He asked me if I was sure. I told him I had a nice evening with the girls and a good sleep.

I needed to go back to London to collect George and my car, in case we needed it during the day. Arriving back in London it was 2am on Saturday morning. I just put my case down and climbed straight into bed, George was fast asleep and I did not want to wake him. I woke at about 8am, then George woke, he found me on the kitchen floor crying. I just could not believe William had gone. For the first few days I told George 'I cannot go back and say goodbye.' I wanted to remember my night in the hospital with William and the times he told me he loved me, but deep down knew I would regret it. I called Matthew on the Tuesday and he said George and I could stay with him, so Wednesday at 4pm we set off, arriving in Hull at 9.20pm. I could not drive past the family home as I had always done in the past.

Mary, her husband and son stayed with Edward. I could not even bear to see them the night before the service. Morning came; I awoke at 4.30am, my stomach churning. The day had arrived and I knew it was going to be a sad one. I sat in the garden listening to the birds and repeating I love you William, looking up at the clouds.

George and I went straight to the church, I could not leave from William's home, I could not get in the car and watch him being driven away in a coffin. It still did not feel real to me that he had gone. It touched my heart to see how many people had turned out to say goodbye to him, then I turned and saw the pall-bearers walking through the beautiful, floral paved garden, I watched as my sister in-law and two daughters got out of the car along with Mary, James also went straight to the church, he said the same as me, he could not follow the coffin to the church.

Once inside, the music started to play; 'I'm half way to paradise', there was a photo of William placed in front of the coffin and I never took my eyes off him, all the way through the service he seemed to be looking straight back at me, with that beautiful smile. Then they played 'The Wonder of You', the tears started to flow; I cannot get it out of my mind how much he had suffered. My heart shaped flowers with 'Sleep peacefully William with Mam and Dad' were laid on top of the coffin. The service was beautiful and as the last song was played, 'Diana,' I shouted out, 'I will never forget you William. I love you brother and thank you for everything you did for me.'

My sister in-law had requested for the curtains not be closed till everyone was outside the church, looking back it was best for everyone, especially James and I, we would have walked out of the church, plus watching them close would really have torn me apart. Before we walked out of the church I went to his photo and kissed him on the lips. 'I love you William, no more suffering,' I said, 'you are with Mam and Dad now, and they will take care of you.' I believe they had been looking down on all of us, but Dad told Mam, 'Come on Sally, William has suffered enough, let's go and get him.'

George and I said we would not go to the reception afterwards, we were going to find a bed and breakfast in Beverley and stay the night, but the family insisted so we went back.

'Ok, just the one then.'

We said we would hit the motorway, but it turned out that Edward had asked George if we wanted to stay with him that night. Later on we went back to Edward's and that evening myself, George, Edward and his partner went for a meal. It was nice because we sat and talked about William and remembered everything he had done for us as children.

Mary embraced me outside the church, it was William's day so I did not want any deep family discussions. She told me I am so different but she loved me. How could I be different? We came from the same womb and should have shared the same love. To me the only difference is we grow up to be adults and have our own families, but should never forget our siblings (charity starts at home). If a member of the family is financially better off than another, perhaps because of a career path they have chosen, everyone should be aware that material things are not important but some are; daily essentials and if a family member suffers ill health through no fault of their own, all families should pull together and try and ease their pain. Some people survive cancer, some don't and it's the same with diabetes. It depends on the strength and their internal organs and when people say they do not help themselves, they are ignorant and it makes me very angry (babies for example are born with such horrible diseases). Medical professionals cannot cure the problem, so how does an individual? As much as you exercise and eat healthy, if the disease wants to take you it will. You must live your life one day at a time, the next day I went back to the church and put flowers on Mam's resting place. I said, 'One day William, we will all be together again, so till then walk through God's garden. Holding Mam and Dad's hands, free from pain, I was so proud to call you brother.'

Dedication

I dedicate this book to my brothers for staying around when things got really tough and for looking out for Mam and I, especially William who helped provide for us during what should have been happier times.

I would like to thank Matthew my cousin for taking Mam to visit Dewsbury where she could remember the happy times with her own mother during the war.

To my husband George for giving me the perfect marriage and providing me with a good life and the home my mother never had.

But most of all, I dedicate this book to my Mam for the courage she showed, no matter what life threw at her, she would never let go.

Today you have two choices: you either stay and put up with domestic violence and verbal abuse, or you walk away. In the sixties there were no organisations to help the women and children who suffered, thankfully there are today.